This book belongs to

_____

_____

Christine Thompson-Wells
Author, Qualified Professional, Accredited Educator &
Independent Writer
BA Education, Dip of Teaching, MACEA

We support Diabetes Type One & Motor Neuron Disease. 10% of the net sales
will be divided equally between both charities.

Our Mission:

Every child and adult have value and is important to us; therefore, we strive through online education and book publishing, to bring life skill education to all children and all families.

For Education Packages

See our book websites: www.how2books.com.au and
www.fullpotentialtraining.com.au
or Contact:
admin@fullpotentialtraining.com.au

HORMONES WITH HATS

MEETING CURRICULUM OBJECTIVES – UNITED KINGDOM (UK)

Natural body changes for boys between School Years 7 to 9, ages 11 to 14 years.

(Health and Wellbeing, Relationships, and Living in the Wider World)

Relationships Education, Relationships and Sex Education (RSE) and Health Education.

'Effective RSE does not encourage early sexual experimentation. It should teach young people to understand human sexuality and to respect themselves and others. It enables young people to mature, build their confidence and self-esteem and understand the reasons for delaying sexual activity. Effective RSE also supports people, throughout life, to develop safe, fulfilling, and healthy sexual relationships, at the appropriate time.'[1]

CURRICULUM OBJECTIVES – AUSTRALIA

Incorporating and supporting Year 7-9, ages 11-14 years. Personal, Social and Community Health (ACPPS070 – ACPS076 - ACPPS071 - ACPPS072 - ACPPS073 – and other related areas of the Curriculum including: TLF-IDM021182 Scootle.edu.au). For School and family packages, please see Pages 109 - 110 for further information.

---

[1] Relationships and Sex Education (RSE) (Secondary) - GOV.UK (www.gov.uk) Extracted from 'statutory guidance Relationships Education, Relationships and Sex Education (RSE) and Health Education & Australia: https://www.scootle.edu.au

If you have purchased this book without its cover, it may be a stolen book.

Neither the publisher or the author is under any obligation to provide professional services in anyway, legal, health or in any form which is related to this book, its contents advice or otherwise.

The law and practices vary from country to country and state to state.

If legal or professional information is required, the purchaser, or the reader should seek the information privately and best suited to their particular needs, and circumstances.

This is not a medical book. It is a book developed by the publisher to open the conversation about how the human body changes when growing up.

The author and publisher specifically disclaim any liability that may be incurred from the information within this book.

All rights reserved. No part of this book, including the interior design, images, cover design, diagrams, or any intellectual property (IP), icons and photographs may be reproduced or transmitted in any form by any means (electronic, photocopying, recording or otherwise) without the prior permission of the publisher. ©

Copyright© 2022 MSI Australia

All rights reserved.

ISBN: 978-0-6451314-0-6

Published by How2Books
Under licence from MSI Ltd, Australia
Company Registration No: 96963518255
NSW, Australia

See our website: www.how2books.com.au
Or contact by email: sales@how2books.com.au
Covers and Copyright owned by MSI, Australia

MSI acknowledges the author and images, text and photographs used in this book.

Children's books

Will Jones Space Adventures & The Money Formula – Book
Will Jones Space Adventures & The Money Formula – The Play
Will Jones & The Money Formula – Educator's Resource Pack
Will Jones Space Adventures & the Zadrilian Queen – Book
Will Jones Space Adventures & The Zadrilian Queen – Play
Will Jones Space Adventures & The Zadrilian Queen – Educator's Resource Pack
There are many more Will Jones Books To Come Out
Dora Damper Makes Honey Damper Bread
Potato Pete Goes to Market
Changes Facing Rosie
Changes Facing Kian
Changes Facing Jai
Changes Facing Caitlin

Books For Adults

Devils In Our Food
Recipes Without Devil Additives
How To Reduce Stress – Find Your Positive Head Space
Making Cash Flow
Selling Made Easy
Know Your Destination 'Go' Learn To Drive Your Mind
The Golden Book Of Whispering Poems and many more books.
Please see our website

Disclaimer

This is not a medical book and should not be used as such. The contents have been developed through observational theory and research (observational psychology). Information is also drawn from scientific literature, web search and personal enquiry.

The diagrams are for information and to enhance the meaning of the written text. Statements, information, and ideas within this book are for education purposes only. The text presented allows the reader to draw their own conclusions on the content offered.

Always consult with your doctor for possible illness or underlying illness. Christine Thompson-Wells (MSI) Australia, How2Books.com.au and Full Potential Training.com.au, cannot be held liable for any errors or omissions.

PREFACE

The characters and story within this book are fictitious. If a similar name or identity is drawn from within the writing, it is purely coincidental. The stories are not representative of any one or more individuals. The stories come together through my own unique and individual teaching and life experiences that are brought together to create this book.

Because all children worldwide go through similar bodily changes at similar times growing up, the stories connect with different children worldwide. The places where children are living are used to ground the story. The locations are destinations I have visited on my own life journey.

Each book targets different age and growth spans, and the story base incorporates children's stories, taking into account, some artistic thought, and writing.

The four books (two for boys and two for girls) are within the series: 'Changes', Children Growing Up, have been designed in a narrative form: (story telling) to assist children and to allow them to naturally adapt to their environment while they go through the different child to adult stages.

It is with sensitivity, that I acknowledge different cultures and traditions, this, and to my best ability, is understood in the writing, illustrations, and storytelling.

HOW TO USE THIS BOOK

In a NEW and exciting approach, hormone characters help our children learn about how their body changes when growing up.

The chapters are the story book. This approach allows the young adult to come to grips with how their body and the way they think is changing.

Part Two introduces the adults to the story and the information the young person has learnt and how respect needs to work in all relationships.

Part Three allows both the young adult and older adults to work through the pages together. This process helps the family to celebrate the changes that all young people go through as they go into adulthood. By 'opening up' the conversation, young adults gain self-esteem, become ready for the changes their body is about to make, and become confident young people enjoying their journey into adulthood.

Part Four identifies the significance of how their brain, maturity and knowledge of the essential responsibilities that being a young adult brings into their life. By identifying, Involvement, Structure, Recall, Production, and Harvesting, then onto Consent, Friendship, Communication and Understanding, we are equipping our young adults with not only knowledge, but the social skills needed to confidently navigate into their future.

Part Five identifies how some hormones change the way the body reacts to different hormones; some hormones can lead to skin outbreaks and other skin irritations. This part helps the young adult to know how hygiene and care can, not only make them feel good, but add to their overall wellbeing.

Part Six is the journey that identifies how many young people have the desire to 'stretch their wings' and commit to different life challenges.

We encourage both boys and girls to read these books.

Christine

Contents

	Page
Preface	
How To Use This Book	
'CHANGES' Children Face Difficult Times – From Child to Adult	
Let's Re-cap	
Introduction	
CHAPTER ONE	1
The Friendship of Two Boys	
CHAPTER TWO	10
A New Term and High School Begins	
CHAPTER THREE	19
Learning More About Hormones	
CHAPTER FOUR	31
How Hormones Help to Change the Human Body	
CHAPTER FIVE	37
Meeting With Aunty Betty	
CHAPTER SIX	53
The Rites of Passage into Manhood	
PART TWO	71
Working Together – For Young Adults and their Family RESPECT	
PART THREE	76
Working Together – For Young Adults and their Family OPENING UP THE CONVERSATION – CONTINUING THE JOURNEY	
PART FOUR	87
Working Together – For Young Adults and their Family INVOLVEMENT, STRUCTURE, RECALL, PRODUCTION and HARVESTING – CONSENT, FRIENDSHIP, COMMUNICATION, UNDERSTANDING YOUR BOY, BUILDING HIS SKILL BASE AND WORKING WITH HIS AMAZING BRAIN	
PART FIVE	98
Working Together – For Young Adults and their Family HYGEINE and CARE	
PART SIX	103
Working Together – For Young Adults and their Family A TIME of LEARNING and GROWTH	
UNDERSTAND HOW THE HUMAN BODY GROWS AND and MATURES	107
Online School Packages	108
Online Family Packages	109

We pay our respects to the original people and traditional owners of Bulahdelah, also known as Worimi, which means the meeting of two rivers in Australian Aboriginal language.

'CHANGES'

CHILDREN FACE DIFFERENT SITUATIONS – FROM A CHILD TO AN ADULT

Facing the changes that the human body and brain go through are just some of the differences that all children go through as they go into adulthood.

Differences identified

Each stage of a child's life is similar but not the same, however, there are markers that will allow both young and older adults to identify different differences as the child develops:

0 – 6 or 7 years – a child is committed to their family and those people who care for them.

7 – 11 years - a child starts to form their own identity and becomes aware; they also have an opinion and want to be heard.

11 – 13 or 14 years – a child, now a young adult, will show different attitudes to different situations and may become opinionated about their own beliefs and boundaries.

14 – 25 years – the young adult will want to try different experiences and may test their environment; it can be a stressful time for loved ones or those onlookers such as grandparents, siblings, and close people within the family.

Facing the differences between the ages of 13 – 14 and up until 25 years can be daunting without a child being guided through that time. It has been seen in many generations, how customs and traditions within many cultures, have been established over many thousands of years, and how to help both children and their parents cope over these times.

Having said the above, maturity and development in some males may come at a later stage and age than females. Testosterone, personality structure and life experiences all play their part in how, and when a young person becomes a mature adult.

Life experiences and how a person is treated as a child all influence the formation of the brain, the personality creation, and the behaviours shown as the young adult matures.

From my own experiences, the ages from 14 years through to about 25 years seem to be the most stressful for a parent. Not only as parents, do we struggle with our own emotions and of letting go, and letting go we must, our children may take on the world as if there is no tomorrow; they test, test and test, sometimes with negative results and then still test again!

LET'S RECAP

In the first two books: Changes Facing Kian and Changes Facing Rosie, I introduced the children to eight different hormones, the growth hormone (HGH), estrogen, progesterone, testosterone, estrone, estradiol, estriol and ghrelin.

The hormones within our bodies help to keep us healthy and allow us to live our daily lives. Hormones are essential if the body is to perform different movements, make different choices and to let us know when to eat, drink, fight, or flight; they are an essential part of the living system in animals, insects, and human beings.

To grow and be healthy, we need HGH within our body. When your body grows, you know you are getting older and growing into an adult.

HGH works with the other hormones we have within our body. None of the hormones working to keep you healthy, can function properly, if you don't eat the correct food that your body identifies. Your food is the primary source of nutrition that feeds your hormones. When hormones have good food, so does your nervous system, your brain and body.

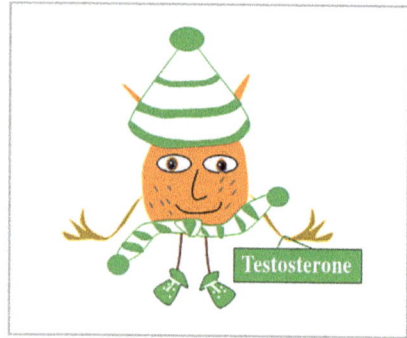

Testosterone, both males and females produce testosterone in their body, but males generally make more than females.

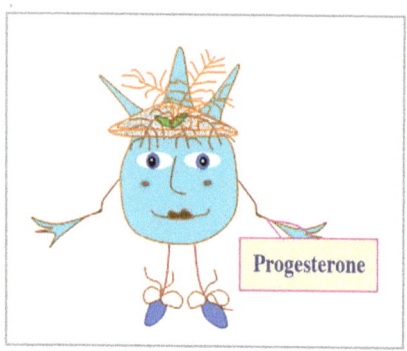

Progesterone is a hormone produced and released from the female ovaries. It helps when females start to have their periods and they help in the body's control of the menstrual cycle.

Estrone can store estrogen and helps with female development and plays a part in female reproductive health. Like most hormones, these work with your body's clock. Many hormones can be sensitive to your body changes. An example may be seen with severe dieting without medical advice or guidance.

Estriol, like estrone, and estradiol, helps the female body to grow and become ready for womanhood. Like so many hormones, it too, works with its own clock and will click into gear when it receives certain messages from your brain.

Estradiol is also a female hormone, produced primarily in the female ovaries. Estradiol levels can vary depending on the phase of the female menstrual cycle. Males also produce estradiol in their body.

Estrogen is the name given to a group of hormone compounds. It is a main hormone and is essential to the menstrual cycle which can go from twenty-one to thirty-five days. Estrogen helps a girl's body to mature. It also helps to make the bones stronger, and to keep the heart and brain healthy.

Women and girls have three types of hormones that work within the reproductive menstrual cycle: estrogen, estradiol and estriol. Estrogen binds together estradiol and estriol. Both males and females have this hormone.

Ghrelin is the hormone that lets you know when you feel hungry. If people eat when they are not hungry, for instance, junk food can make you feel full and about an hour later after the meal, you feel hungry again. This is when your ghrelin hormone is being overridden by the food additives in junk and processed food!

Hormones work as communication transmitters and can switch different chemicals on or off within the body and brain.

To give you some idea of this, when a tiny baby is hungry,

the hunger message is sent from the child's stomach to its brain. Ghrelin is thought to be produced in the stomach and has a direct communication route to the brain, a bit like a telecom's transmitter! The message is sent from the stomach through the nervous system that runs along the spine, to the brain. The reaction comes from the baby by the sound of the cry it makes!

The sound of the cry allows a mother to instantly understand the message, 'I am hungry!'

NOW, MORE HORMONES THAN YOU REALISE!

INTRODUCTION

This is the second book in the series of two books for boys. 'Changes' Facing Kian, now we bring to you, 'Changes' Facing Jai.

This is a story about a boy from India who lives in Bulahdelah, NSW, Australia, with his mum and dad.

His best friend, Nullah, also lives in the town with his Aboriginal and First Australian nation family. Jai and Nullah, befriend an Australian boy, of a similar age who has recently come to live in Bulahdelah.

When the three boys go on their bike rides, they learn a lot from Nullah, about the Australian bush, and the animals that live in their natural habitat.

Each boy learns from their friends as they enter the journey of puberty. Coming into the story is Great Aunty Betty, an Aboriginal Elder and professional doctor who runs her own practice in the town.

Within the story, respect is paid to the cultural background of all three boys, it does however, highlight, some of the difficulties that some children face when their parents are struggling in their marriage; this situation is identified, when the new boy Nick, joins the two friends later in the story.

With the emphasis on puberty and the young male's changing body, respect is very much a part of the book's content. The introduction of many hormones allows the boys to learn about 'how?' and 'why?' puberty happens at similar ages to all children across the world.

Chapter One
The friendship of two boys

Jai is a migrant boy from India. He and his family have lived in Australia for the last seven years; he has all the Australian traits that other Australian children have regarding the Australian culture and way of life.

He lives in Bulahdelah, is a member of the local football club and has a lot of Australian friends including, Nullah. Nullah is a First Nation, Australian, who lives with his mum, dad and younger brother and has constant contact with his people.

The boys are the same age, have a similar build in body weight and height. Jai has green eyes and Nullah's are deep brown.

The boys go to the same school, have similar interests and their families often meet up at social events. Nullah's and Jai's dad often meet when the boys are playing football; each boy plays for a different side, so there can be some rivalry between the dads!

When the boys first meet at school, they instantly like each other and have been best friends since that time. Jai's birthday is in May, and Nullah's in June; they usually celebrate their birthdays' together.

The boys were now getting older and were going to the same high school at the beginning of the next school year. The boys had shared their last birthdays together with both families joining for a large family barbecue.

It is now summertime, and Australia has had more torrential rain than normal. After many years of drought, the rain is welcome. The rivers start to fill to capacity, the foliage, and grasses in the national parks around Bulahdelah are lush and green and the trees are sprouting new growth.

It was a perfect time for Jai and Nullah to go out on their bikes. The boys didn't have new bikes, just bikes that had been reclaimed from the re-cycled bike shop and given the once over by Nullah's dad! Nullah's dad wanted to make sure they were road worthy and wouldn't let the boys down when they were riding out in the bush!

It is early one morning during the school summer holidays and Nullah meets Jai at his house. Nullah was ready to go, and Jai had to get out of bed quickly when he heard Nullah's voice outside his bedroom window, *'Jai, are you up, don't you remember we are going out for our ride?'*

Jai was still waking up as he got dressed; his clothes were still on the floor from the day before! Before putting them on, he looked out of his window, and waved to his friend. Nullah knew that Jai would be quick.

Once dressed, Jai ran through the kitchen, his mum had made some Naan bread the night before and left it on top of the oven to cool. Seeing the bread, Jai pulled some of the delicious food apart and stuffed it into his pocket.

Both boys were now on their bikes and heading up the road and into the National Park. They got to the park, where Nullah signalled to Jai to stop riding, he did this. Being a little way behind, Jai was now alongside Nullah. Jai had forgotten about his delicious bread and as he put his hand into his pocket, he realised and then pulled the bread out offering Nullah half.

Nullah had eaten Indian Naan bread before and loved the taste of the food.

The boys stood with their bikes leaning between their legs, they were looking at the amazing mountain ahead of them, while they continued eating their breakfast!

Both boys saw the blue sky, the white floating clouds as they caressed the mountain summit, the greyish colours of the rocks against the greens of the grasses and native ferns, and the grey and green gum tree leaves with the shining grey trunks of some native species. They could also see spots of yellow where the last of the wattle still needed to come into full flower.

As they stood and enjoyed their food, Nullah stopped and said to Jai, *'Do you hear that?'* Jai stopped chewing, scratched his head, and then listened again, he heard the birds but mainly he could hear, in the far distance, the sounds of Bell birds. He nodded his head back to Nullah. He had never heard that sound before and could not think of anything more beautiful.

Though it was daylight, the sun had not fully risen and both boys knew it was very early in the morning. The people of Bulahdelah, including the boys' families, would still be in their beds asleep!

The boys having finished their food continued riding their bikes up the mountain. The ground was rocky and steep but still the boys rode over largish rocks and sometimes they would find a dirt track which made the journey easier.

Meanwhile back at Jai's home, his mum was now up. She walked into the kitchen and looked at her bread, now with only half of it left in tack, she knew instantly that Jai would be out on his bike with Nullah.

She felt a bit annoyed with her son because he was told, *'if people aren't home or if you go out early in the morning when we are all asleep, you must leave a note telling us where you are going and who you are going with and what time you will be home!'*

She instantly walked into Jai's bedroom and there on his unmade bed was his note to his mum and family. He had done exactly what his mum had asked. On seeing the note written on wrinkled and crumpled paper with Jai's writing, she picked it up and saw his message. He had done exactly what she had told him to do!

Nullah had also left his home early and his mum also went into his bedroom, Nullah shared his room with his younger brother Charlie, Charlie had seen Nullah go and said, '*…mum, Nullah has left you a message on his bed!*' As he spoke to his mum, Charlie, wiped his heavy eyelids with the knuckles of his fingers removing the sleep from his eyes!

Nullah's mum hadn't made bread the night before because her baking day was today. But before she did that, she needed to get busy because she was helping at the charity shop. She thinks, 'I will take Charlie with me, he can help to tidy up those boxes sitting in the corner by the clothes bins.' She thinks again, 'I also want to speak to the ladies in my painting group!'

Charlie knew, because he was a lot younger than Nullah, he would have to go with his mum. He didn't mind going to the charity shop because there was always lots of things to do. Sometimes he would attach labels to toys, this was done by him sticking the labels on the toys and an adult would write its price on the label so that it could be sold in the shop.

He had mastered this skill and before the toys went into the shop, he had the chance to play with them! It wasn't only the toys that amused Charlie, he loved reading books, and so helping his mum, allowed him to see any books that came to the store. This part of the day he loved. He would sometimes find a place between the clothes bins, sit, snuggled down between the bins, and read for hours!

With his time spent in the shop, he had the opportunity to see, not only new books, but puzzles, fishing rods, and so many items, that may be sold in the shop, once they were inspected by the manager!

At morning tea, Mrs Fisher, who lived in the same street as Nullah and his family, would treat Charlie to a small banana milk shake. 'She only ever bought small amounts of anything...!' was Charlie's thoughts. Mid-morning, she would go and buy herself a small coffee for morning tea, she would say on returning from the coffee shop, '...*my treat for the week...!*' and on giving the milkshake to Charlie, she would continue, '...*only a small one today, I don't want to spoil your lunch....!*' Charlie didn't mind, he just loved the milk shake...!

As it was school holidays, the shop was busy with many visitors, coming into the town! Some, looking for bargains, some looking to buy something different, and some didn't buy anything! Charlie would sit behind the counter, while he sucked the milkshake through a straw, from its container. He watched the different people from different parts of the country and some, from different parts of the world!

As Charlie saw many different people in the shop, all, of the time, Charlie would sit watching and enjoy the moment!

He didn't think about Nullah and Jai at these times because he was busy doing his own thing. His mum was in the back of the shop working and sorting out clothes, shoes, toys, and other things that needed either throwing away, going to the recycled bin, or if there were any other uses for it or them?

One thing that Charlie's mum loved was the glass crystal that was brought in for re-sale. When she found a piece, she would look at it and ask Charlie, *'What do you think Charlie, should I buy that….?'* Charlie had no idea, he just knew that his mum had so much glass at home and if she bought more, he asked himself, '…where would she put it…?'

This time, while he sat behind the counter drinking his banana milkshake, his mum came out of the back room where she had been working. She had a coloured glass dish in her hand and Charlie instantly knew she was going to ask for his opinion. Charlie being only six, knew that his mum could put fruit into the dish but that is all that he knew.

Charlie's mum had a big smile on her face and was excited. She made her way to her son while carrying the dish. She looked down at Charlie as he sat on the low stool, and said, *'What do you think, Charlie, do you think your dad and Nullah would like this?* His reply, *'I don't know mum…!'*

Charlie's mum turned, walked away with her newly found glass dish and says back to her son while still walking towards the backroom doorway: *'I will think about buying it. Don't go out into the street, stay behind the counter where Mrs. Fisher can keep an eye on you and make sure you behave and do as you are told, also be good!'*

Charlie thought to himself, 'Mum says that every time she comes into the shop...!'

Meanwhile, Nullah and Jai are enjoying their bike ride up Bulahdelah Mountain. Partway up the mountain, Nullah is a little way in front of Jai, and stops riding his bike, Jai sees his friend and once close enough, he too stops riding. Each, with one leg dangling and secured by the crossbar of the bike, the boys start to talk, drink from their water bottles, and enjoy the bush sounds.

They can feel the sun as it starts to go higher into the sky; it is starting to get very warm, and the boys decide to keep riding up the mountain side.

Nullah says, *'Jai, this is a very special place for Aboriginal people and our ancestors have always respected this place….'* Jai listens with interest as Nullah continues, *'This is a place where the animals can live safely, and the plants and trees can grow without being picked or cut down...!'* As Jai listens to his friend, he becomes interested in the history and story of the mountain.

Jai takes the time to listen to the birds talking to each other, the sounds of the gum leaves, as they rustle together, with sharpened, and insect eaten edges, make them sound like they are speaking their own 'leaf language'. This is all happening in the early morning breeze and the gentle feeling of the new sun rays as they hit his skin. He then thinks, '...this is indeed a very special place...!'

The boys return to their journey and follow a narrow pathway cut through the bush by previous walkers in the area; the way ahead is very narrow and steep!

As the boys' ride, Jai sees different marks and carved pictures carved into the wood of the trees. He has never seen anything just like this before! He thinks about the people who may have carved them. But his thoughts are broken as Nullah says, '*...see Jai. if you look through the trees, you can see the lakes down there.*' Jai looks, and he sees the landscape of distant water, birds flying, and close by, the butterflies are flying from plant to plant gathering nectar. Nullah again, says, '*...those butterflies are good, they help to pass the pollen from flower to flower, that's what my grandad told me last week!*'

Chapter Two
A new term and high school begins

After the long bike ride up the Bulahdelah Mountain, and when Jai returned home that day, Jai's mum was busy in the kitchen preparing food for the evening meal. He could also hear the drum and thud, the drum and thud of the washing machine in the laundry as it was one of his mum's washing days in the week.

Jai's mum was glad to see her son, she welcomes him with a light pinch on the cheek of his face. With this action, he always knew his mum had something extra to say….!

She looks at Jai squarely in the face and says, '*…now Jai, you know we have a rule in this house, can you remember that rule?* Jai, sheepishly replies, '*…yes, mama.*' She then says, '*…and what is that rule?*' He replies, '*The first thing to be done once I'm out of bed, is to make my bed….!*' She is standing in front of him with her hands on her hips and is nodding her head…! She replies, '*Yes, my son, you must always make your bed and then your mind is ready to make a good day!*'

Jai's mum wears a traditional Indian dark dress while she does her housework, washing and cooking. Her going out dresses are very colourful; she feels very special when she wears one of her latest outfits she has sent from India. Jai's dad, when he sees how beautiful his wife is looking, always comments and tells her, '*You look so glamourous in your new clothes.*' He will also tell his wife, '*You look beautiful!*' Jai's mum usually becomes embarrassed by his comments but deep inside, she enjoys the flirting and flattery.

With his mother's words ringing in his ears, Jai, goes to his room to make his bed and tidy the room, including putting his dirty washing in the washing basket. He then decides to take some time out to sit in the garden and a time to think about his experiences on the bike ride up the mountain with Nullah.

Some weeks had passed since the boys had gone on their bike ride and it was now time to start a new term and a new school.

Jai hadn't realised at the time, but the bike rides up the mountain with Nullah had made a difference to him and it had made a difference to how he saw himself and how he saw his new country.

His family loved Australia and loved living in Bulahdelah, however, they never forgot where they had come from, and the love, they still had for their home country!

It was Friday afternoon, and both the girls and boys had their own football games on that afternoon. The girls played their game first while the boys watched on and then the boys played.

Nullah and Jai were on different sides and that caused both their dads to cheer their respective team on. The game was going well. Jai is not a great sportsman, but he was playing well today, and Jai's dad was very proud of his son. The two dads would meet at the gate of the sportsground and give each other a gentle elbow nudge when one of the boys did something good and unexpected!

Jai now had the ball; he was moving quickly across the field keeping the ball just in front of the toe of his boot; his dad had never seen anything like it. Jai could sense that Nullah was close, but he didn't realise just how close...!

With the flick of the toe of his boot, Nullah took the ball from Jai, the crowd was shouting and cheering. Jai was quickly back on Nullah and was determined to chase the ball! Both boys seem to be playing their own game with the rest of the team left far behind! From one to the other, up and down the pitch, the ball was exchanged, as both boys took each other on.

The supporters were going mad; they had not seen the two boys play football like this ever. Eventually, Nullah scored the winning goal.

After the game, Jai's dad came up to him and said, *'Son, I have never seen you play like that.'* Then Nullah and Nullah's dad also came up to Jai and his dad. The dads stood patting the boys on their heads and singing their praises.

When Jai got home that night, Jai's dad could not believe what he had seen. With great excitement over the evening meal, Jai's dad told the story again and again. He was still laughing and thumping his chest with pride as he ate his meal.

Eventually, Jai's mum said, *'Ali, would you please stop talking about the football match. The boys played very well but we have other things to talk about. Your sister will be here tomorrow, and I need to ask you about the barbecue you are planning for the family!'*

Jai's dad briefly stopped talking for a bit. He listened to what his wife had to say, got up from the table and as he did, said, *'I will get the barbecue out and give it a clean.'* Jai's mum watched her husband as he walked out of the room, with that, he looked back at Jai with a smile all over his face, then replied, *'brilliant game, you played so well my son, I'm so proud of you….!'* Jai's mum shook her head and then said to Jai, *'…please clear the table, put everything back into the fridge and cupboard and then you can go and help your dad. He will want to keep talking about the football match, so you had better be the one to hear him!'*

The following Monday, the Head Teacher mentioned the football game in the assembly and Jai felt embarrassed as his and Nullah's names were called out. Then the other students clapped for them. That too, Jai felt embarrassed about. On the other hand, Nullah loved the fuss and the commendations he was receiving.

Nullah and Jai met for lunch; they knew a new kid had joined the school. Neither Nullah nor Jai knew this student!

During their lunch break and while sitting on the grass under the trees, an unfamiliar boy with an unfamiliar face walked towards them!

He was very well dressed and very polite when he asked, '*Do you mind if I join you?*' Both Jai and Nullah moved along a bit on the ground giving the new boy some of their grass space to sit on.

The boys continue to introduce themselves to each other and then the siren goes to tell them, the lunch break is over.

A few days went by before Nullah, and Jai saw the new student again. This time, they were all making their way to an afternoon assembly for an announcement. The new student had introduced himself as Nick. After the assembly, Nick caught up with Nullah and Jai. He wanted to chat.

As the three boys had walked to school that morning, they were on foot; this gave them a perfect opportunity to get to know each other. It was a downhill walk to town from the school. Jai was meeting his mum at the supermarket to help her with the grocery shopping and Nullah was meeting his mum at the charity shop where she had several jobs outlined for him to do!

Nick had just moved to Bulahdelah from Sydney. His dad had a contract job in the town for about two years, and then the family would have to move on to the next job. His dad was an engineer '*and works on specific projects…*', he told the two boys.

By this time, the three had reached the town. Nullah went to see his mum and brother, and Jai, met his mum at the supermarket.

While Jai was helping his mum with the shopping, she said, *'Jai, I have something to tell you.'* Jai, stopped to look at his mum, when she announced, *'you are going to have a new brother or sister, I am pregnant!'* Jai didn't really know what to say, but he felt a type of happiness in his stomach and body. He stood closer to his mum and put his arms around her and gave her the hug she would remember for a lifetime.

His next question to his mum was, *'Does dad know?'* She replied, *'I hope so, but yes, he does!'*

The two continued to do the shopping as they went around the supermarket talking to and enjoying each other's company.

Many migrant women have not had the opportunity to learn to drive in their own country, but many are now taking that opportunity while living in Australia. Jai's mum had taken this opportunity and had learnt to drive; she drove everywhere and insisted on driving when Jai's dad wanted to drive. She would say sternly, *'No, Ali, I will drive!'*

The car was loaded with groceries and Jai insisted on carrying every bag from the car to the house for his mum.

It became a regular meeting now with the three boys, Nick would always join his friends, sometimes during the school day. During one of their meetings, Nullah asked, *'Nick, do you have a bike?'* Nick replied, *'I do, but I will need to pump the tyres up as I haven't ridden my bike since we left Sydney!'*

Nullah suggested the three boys meet on Sunday afternoon for a bike ride up the mountain. Nick quickly responded, *'...that sounds great, yes, I'd like to do that!'*

That same afternoon, the three boys all met, with the other students, in the large classroom at the back of the school. The lesson was on Children Growing Up.

Jai had been dreading the lesson, but now that his mum and dad were expecting another baby, he thought, 'I should learn as much about this stuff as I can, now that I'm going to have a brother or sister...!'

The teacher came from another school to give the lesson and started by introducing her name; she was Mrs Zayed.

The first thing she wanted to talk about were hormones. The mention of the word hormones surprised Jai. He thought the teacher would want to talk about other more embarrassing things, like the human body and how parts of the body grow and change shape! But she did not, 'at least during this lesson', he thinks...!

She starts the lesson, saying, '*I recognise some of you students, you were in my classes last year. First, I want to briefly speak about some of the hormones before going on to the new ones I want to speak about. Sometimes, I will go back and speak about the hormones you learnt about last year while I introduce the new ones!*'

The teacher continues, '*...to allow for people and animals to grow, and for the species to survive, they must grow to maturity. All growing things need a growth hormone for this to happen.*' She takes a breath, while pointing at the image on the screen and continues, '*The growth hormone is also known as (HGH) or hGH. This is a naturally occurring hormone produced by the pituitary gland, it stimulates growth into maturity in children and continues to work in young adults during adolescents. The pituitary gland sits in and works from the middle of your brain.*'

She then says, '*If you put your finger, and in your mind, think of a line on top and in the middle of your head and then imagine where the front of your ear is, then think about meeting the two lines, within the middle of your brain, you will roughly understand*

where the two lines meet is where your pituitary gland sits within your brain! Please look at this image!'

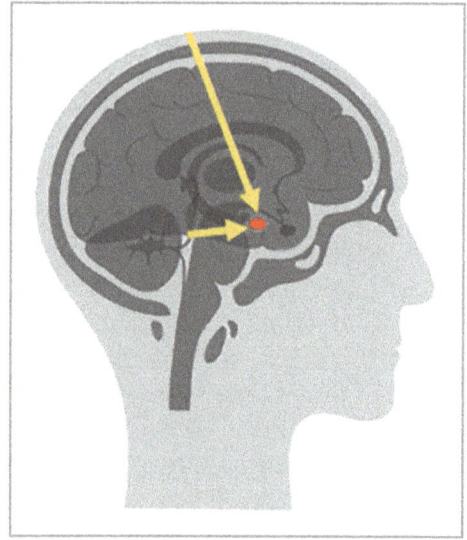

The teacher stopped speaking while the students did the exercise of trying to draw the imaginary lines with their fingers on their heads!

There were about thirty students in the room and with each student working from the top of their heads to their front of their ears, the laughter and good learning being done was great for the teacher to see.

Nullah and Nick took out their rulers to measure their heads while Jai tried to draw a picture of his head which included his ears. He then drew the lines, using his set square, so that he could see how the lines would meet and to roughly estimate where *his pituitary gland sits within his brain!*

Chapter Three
Learning more about hormones

After the lesson on hormones, Sunday afternoon came around quickly, and the boys meet at the café in town before making their way up the mountain.

It was a hot day; the boys fill their water bottles at the fountain in the park before heading off on their bike ride. Nick hadn't ridden his bike for a long time, so every now and again, he would stop, have a drink of water, and then catch the boys up! The three were at the foot of the mountain and the sun was high in the sky at about two o'clock in the afternoon. Nullah suggested they all sit under a large tree for a while before heading off onto, and up the mountain track.

They were sitting on the ground enjoying the shade of the trees leaves when Nullah heard a rustle and slithering sound in the grasses and fallen leaves behind them! Nullah, knew from his dad and grandad, that the sound was of a large snake coming their way. Nullah, stopped the boys from talking and they all listened. Jai was not aware of what he was listening for, and Nick had no idea of the bush! To stop Nick from saying anything, Nullah put his index finger up to his mouth, which said silence to both boys.

As Nullah did this, the largest brown snake Nullah had ever seen slid past the boys while they sat and watched it turn, see them, and then head off in another direction!

Nullah looked at his friends, and with a deep breath, said, '...*that is the biggest brown I have ever seen; my dad won't believe it when I tell him!*'

Once the snake was on its way and well out of view, the boys got onto their bikes and resumed their ride up the mountain. As the vegetation became thicker, the heat of the day lessened, and the boys continued their ride.

Nullah took his friends a different way this time and Jai saw yet another way of seeing the bush. He was also amazed at the aromas and perfumes of the flowers as he knocked them with his face, as he rode on following Nullah, and occasionally looking back, to see if Nick was still following him! The scent of the eucalyptus and other fragrances made Jai's head spin; he had never witnessed or felt the real nature of the Australian bush before! He thinks, 'even some of the grasses had scents!' Nullah being a little farther ahead, stopped riding and waited for Jai and Nick to catch up! When they did, Nullah showed the boys some edible berries; these were growing next to some inedible berries. Nullah told the boys about what to eat in the bush and what to not eat.

With their botany lesson over, the boys headed off and up to the top of the mountain. This way was a lot steeper than the previous way Jai and Nullah had ridden!

Nick feeling the strain of the ride, got off his bike and continued to walk, and push his bike the rest of the way! There were still rocks and smallish termite mounds to navigate over before the three would reach the summit!

They were almost at the top of the mountain, when Nullah took some time to sit on a large rock and drink some water. The three sat down together; they were all hot and sweaty and each boy found his own comfortable seat.

Jai, said to Nullah and Nick, *'my mum told me last week I'm going to have a baby brother or sister...'* Nullah looked at Nick, while Nick was looking down at some ants making their way backwards and forwards to their nest! He then took a twig and started to annoy the ants, when Nullah warned him, *'...if you annoy them, they will come and pinch you.'* With this warning, Nick then, experienced his first 'ant nip' of the day! Nick screamed out loudly while Nullah and Jai laughed.

Nick standing up, said in a very adult voice, *'when is the baby due?'* Jai replied, *'...don't know, mum hasn't said....!*

Nick still standing nodded his head in reply.

Nullah was now standing and said, *'let's go, we're nearly there!'*

The boys, all thinking their own thoughts, make their way to the summit.

At the summit, the three look out at the views of the lakes and land before them. They sit on the seats of their bikes, drink some water, and continued to look out over the far-reaching landscape. The distance and the late afternoon sun were giving a misty sheen to the grey green, rolling hills.

Nick broke the silence and turned to Jai, and said, *'my mum and dad only had me, I would have liked a brother or sister!'* Once he had made his statement, the three went back to looking straight out before them and to the dulling colours of a hot late afternoon and the slowly fading light of the day! The three boys stood for some time in quiet meditative silence looking at the beauty and the changing colours of the landscape!

Then, Nick said and thinking out loud, *'Mrs Zayed, said we are going to learn more about hormones in the next lesson...!* Nullah replied to Nick's statement, *'...yes, we learnt a bit about those things last year, I really haven't thought about it much, but I can see I'm getting older, and I feel a bit different about lots of things now...!'*

Nick asked, *'...what did you learn about last year?'* As the question was asked, two magnificent hunting birds flew high in the sky, this distracted the boys from their conversation. Nullah quickly identified the birds as wedge-tailed eagles and said, *'there must be something interesting them, they are circling and getting ready to attack!'*

The boys stood watching the birds, circle, and circle in the sky, then, before the boys had time to blink, the birds flew straight down to the ground and up again. Both had a snake each, and wriggle as they might, Nullah explains, '*...you see the birds have the snakes in their talons and without any ground beneath them, the snakes don't have a chance...!'* The three boys watched as the eagles took their prizes off into the far distance...!

Jai asked, '*...what will they do with the snakes?'* Nullah replies, '*...probably feed their chicks if they have any or eat them...!'*

Nick, then breaks up the conversation of the snakes again, and asks about the previous lessons last year from Mrs Zayed. Jai, looks at Nick, then says, '*...you're interested in this stuff, aren't you?'* Nick's reply, '*Yes, it's good to know about your body and how it works...!'* Then Nullah says, '*Our Elders want us to know all this stuff, they say, "...it makes a boy a man when you understand this stuff...!"'*

With Nullah's last comment, the three head back down the mountain and each boy makes his way home and arrives just before it starts to get dark!

The following day was Monday and another school day. Jai, after getting up and making his bed, goes to have his breakfast with his mum and dad.

While sitting at the table and eating, he got up the courage and bravely asked, '*mum, when is the baby due?'* His dad quickly replied, '*Our baby will come in about seven months; your mum and I are looking forward to this.'* With this explanation, Jai's dad reached across the table and held his wife's hand.

Jai decides to ride his bike to school today, on the way, Nullah and Nick catch up to him; the three, while they ride, talk about the eagles and the snakes they saw yesterday!

At school, there was an announcement that Mrs Zayed would come today and not on Wednesday as it had been planned.

The day passed by, and it was time for Mrs Zayed's class. The three boys met at the doorway and when the students were quiet were allowed into the classroom.

Mrs Zayed came into the room and said, *'Good afternoon class, today we will quickly catch up on the information we have done so far, but before I start, are there any questions?'*

Jai, now that his mum was pregnant, wanted to know so much more and wanted to ask so many questions, but he was still a little nervous about asking questions in front of the class!

He got up the courage and said, *'Mrs Zayed, my mum is expecting a baby in about seven months, and I would like to know more about this…!'*

Mrs Zayed was very impressed to hear this comment and said, *'Jai, thank you for letting us know about your* mum, we will definitely learn more about this as we go through the coming weeks.'

Then Nullah, (as though supporting his friend) said, 'it would be good to know this stuff because my mob want us all to know about this...!)

Mrs Zayed, looked relieved and said, 'that is great to hear, Nullah, we can all find out so much when we ask questions and help each other...'

There was a short discussion about hormones and then the class began. Mrs Zayed began her lesson, 'first we spoke about growth hormones and how important they are within everybody's body.' She shows the slides she had shown the class the previous weeks and continues speaking as she does this!

'First there is the Growth hormone (HGH). This hormone is needed to allow your bones to grow and to make you strong.'

She then asks: 'are there any questions?' She waits to see if there are any. She waits and listens to the silence within the room. She then continues.

'Then we spoke about estrogen, and I explained: both males and females have estrogen. In biologically male bodies, estrogen is needed to balance testosterone.' She takes a breath, then continues, '...estrogen also helps to protect your brain, it helps with your memory and in some of the fine jobs it helps the fine muscles in your fingers to work! Such jobs as painting a picture in art; with girls, it helps them when they put on their makeup!

In your technical classes, you may make a fine piece of metal work, this is when estrogen will help you to control how your fingers move with the work you are doing! So, estrogen is very important in our everyday lives. Estrogen also helps when a female's body is ready to make a baby, but as we all know, there are rules and regulations in our community that also need to be obeyed!

Estrogen also helps in the growth of male sperm, so it has many jobs to do...!'

Mrs Zayed now clicks the testosterone slide up onto

the whiteboard and says, 'Testosterone is known as the male hormone and in biologically male bodies, *there is more of this hormone than estrogen. Both boys and girls produce testosterone, but in girls, the amounts are smaller.'* With this comment, some of the boys talk to each other, some laugh, while others sit and wait patiently for the next slide to be seen on the screen.

Mrs Zayed waits for the students to settle down before she begins again. She then continues, *'...all hormones have a job to do. Hormones help your body to stay healthy!'*

There is a lot of chatter in the room and Mrs Zayed again waits patiently for the students to resume their lesson, once settled, she asks the students, *'...are there any questions about the hormones we've discussed so far?'*

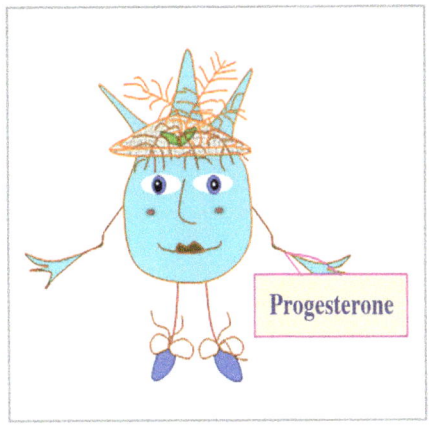

Mrs Zayed continues with the lesson and has the next slide on the screen! She says, *'Both boys and girls produce progesterone.*

Progesterone is known as a master hormone. In females, it is produced in the female ovaries and in the adrenal glands. It is an important hormone. It helps to stop depression, headaches; it also helps in keeping your bones and brain healthy!'

It is mainly seen as a female hormone and is higher when a female is ready to make a baby!'

Mrs Zayed wants to quickly remind her students, she says, 'Class, as I have said previously, there is a lot of responsibility to becoming an adult, and our communities have many rules in place all to do with your responsibilities as an adult!'

Because Jai's mum was now pregnant, he wanted to know more. Nick too showed an interest. Nick puts up his hand to speak, Mrs Zayed, points to Nick and says, 'what do you want to ask Nick?' Nick feels a bit embarrassed as he asks his question, 'Mrs Zayed, you said that boys also make and have progesterone, but boys don't make babies…..!'

With this question, the class falls into raptures of laughter. Mrs Zayed waits for the class to settle down and then continues, 'No, boys don't make babies, but progesterone helps to keep the balance of the hormone testosterone. If there wasn't enough progesterone in the boy's body, they would make too much testosterone and it might make them sick!'

Mrs Zayed waits patiently for any questions about her answer, then continues, 'I am now going to talk about another hormone and that is adrenaline. Amongst other things, adrenaline allows us to stay competitive, play sport, win a competition and to help create an amazing Lego construction and to be the first to finish making a puzzle.' She continues, 'many children are competitive, and competition is good, but competition can cause stress in children and young adults.

We all need to know how to turn off adrenaline.' Mrs Zayed takes a breath, and then continues, 'Having too much adrenaline in our bodies and brains can make us angry and leave us feeling tired!

When we feel like this, we may want to fight with our siblings, cause a fight in the playground, be rude to mum and dad and the people we love. By doing the things we love to do, we can reduce adrenaline, and this makes us feel happy….'

Mrs Zayed, then says, 'Adrenaline is connected to stress; we will talk more about that next week. But before we finish this lesson, I quickly want to introduce you to gonadotropin.'

Just quickly, I want to say, 'Gonadotropins have a main function and that is *to work with the gonads, meaning, the gonad is the sex or reproductive gland in both females and males. The female reproductive cell are egg cells, and in males, the reproductive cells are sperm!'*

With that, the bell for the end of the day went and the children left the classroom!

Chapter Four
How hormones help to change the human body

Jai, Nick and Nullah meet at the bike shed where they each were about to make their way home, before this happens, Nick looks at Nullah and says, *'I didn't realise that hormones were so important in our body.'* Nullah replies, *'Our mob have told me a lot about growing up and have said that my body will change, and I will also start to think differently. When I was talking to my Aunty, she said, if I have any questions, I should ask her?'*

Jai is standing by his bike and listening to his friends. With the last words spoken, the boys head home.

Nullah, on his bike, heads off to his Aunty Betty's house to talk some more about his last school lesson.

She is glad to see her nephew and on seeing him, says, *'You've just missed your mum and brother, your mum was here with her painting group.'* Nullah thinks to himself, nods his head in thank you for knowing his mum and brother were at his aunt's house, and then says to his aunt, *'I want to talk to you about something else!'*

His aunt sensing his wanting to know and enquiry on his face says, *'How about I make us a nice cup of tea and then we can sit and talk?'*

With his hot cup of tea in his hand, he starts to tell his aunt about his last lesson, at this point, he brings out his workbook and shows his aunt the pictures of the hormones.

Nullah's aunt is an elder in the mob and a learned woman having gone to university and trained as a doctor. She looks at the images of the hormones Nullah shows her, she laughs at the faces she sees. She then says, *'It's about time we took the mystery out of growing up!'*

Nullah explains to his Aunty about the information he has learnt so far. He wants to talk frankly and open to her and just as he begins, there is a knock on the door.

She opens it to find Jai and Nick looking at her, she said to them both, *'Welcome, it's nice to see you both; Nullah, and I were just talking about your last lesson!'*

They walk to the back kitchen; she then offers them some tea and then they start to talk about the lesson they had that afternoon.

She starts to talk, taking one hormone at a time:

'Growth hormone, as Nullah has said to me, "helps your bones to grow…" but, it has other benefits also!' She continues, *'…growth hormone or HGH, helps as you grow into men, and as you grow, you will increase your muscle mass, and this reduces your body's fat!'*

'Are there any questions?' she asks. The boys sit quietly, then Jai, over the top of his shirt, feels his arm muscles at the top of his arms; the other two boys follow him to see how their muscles are growing! The four laugh and Aunty, then says, *'shall we continue?'*

'Estrogen is another hormone that we all need. This hormone has different jobs in the body. In females it helps when a woman wants to have a baby. It also helps when a girl starts to develop breasts and like all adults, it helps in allowing pubic hair to grow around the genital area. Some people call this "your private parts" but it is better to call these parts of your body by the real name, the genital area!

Estrogen also helps your brain to stay healthy and for your heart to remain strong. In girls, estrogen helps with regulating her period or menstrual cycle. A period is when a girl releases blood from the vagina; this happens about once a month once a girl reaches a certain age. All girls will start their periods at the time that is right for them!'

She asks the boys, 'are there any questions?' The boys remain silent and interested in what Aunty has to say.

She continues, 'Testosterone is a hormone that needs to be respected. Many people don't understand how this hormone works!' The three boys now pay particular attention to what Aunty has to say.

She continues, 'The boy baby, at about eight weeks into the pregnancy, will start to produce testosterone in the cells of its body. This is the production of the 'Y' chromosome and is made from a chemical the baby's body produces. At this time, the baby will start to grow a penis and testicles; it is not until the baby is about fifteen weeks old, that the testicles and penis are fully formed. Testosterone also makes subtle changes in the brain and body of the baby.

Testosterone allows the baby boy to become stronger as he develops and before his birth.'

Aunty, looks at the boys and studies their faces, she gives them time and then asks, 'do you understand this?' They each nod their head in reply; they do not speak. Aunty looks at them and can see that they are all deeply thinking about the information she has just given them.

She asks, *'would you like to continue, or would you like to come back tomorrow after school?'*

Nullah looks at his watch and says to his Aunty, *'I will come back after school tomorrow, Aunty, what about you Jai and Nick?'* Both Jai and Nick knew it was getting late and agreed, *'Yes, can we come back tomorrow?'* Aunty looked at the boys, and said, *'Of course, this is good learning, and I would love to have you come again!'*

Jai's mum was busy putting food onto the plates when he arrived home. It was also getting late. Jai's mum looked at her son and asked, *'where have you been Jai, I was getting worried?'* Jai apologises to his mum for worrying her. He then says, as his dad comes into the room. When his dad replies, *'You were going to say something Jai?'* Jai is a little embarrassed, but then he decides to tell his mum and dad what he had been doing.

'We went to see Aunty Betty, do you remember, Nullah's dad said about Aunty Betty, she is a trained and qualified doctor, and we had some questions for her, after our Personal Health lesson today. We wanted to know more about hormones...!'

Jai's dad hearing the word *'hormone...'* looked up as he washed his hands in the sink, and in time for dinner, then asked, *'and what did you learn about hormones?'*

At this point, the meal was ready to be eaten and sitting on their plates on the dining room table. Jai, thought to himself, '...this subject will have to wait for another opportunity...!'

The next day and after breakfast, Jai's dad quickly reminded his son of the conversation they were going to have the night before, *'Don't forget Jai, we were having a conversation about hormones last night. I will be home early, so we can talk...!'*

At that point, he opened the front door and walked to the garage to get into his car to drive to work! Jai stands on the front step while his dad drives onto the main road and waves to him as his dad passes by.

The boys now meet in the school playground, secure their bikes in the bike rack, and head off to their respective classes. During morning break, Jai tells the boys, *'I won't be able to see Aunty Betty tonight as I've made arrangements with my dad to talk about the lesson on hormones.'*

Nick replies, *'I didn't say anything to my parents, they aren't getting on too well now! If I'm honest, life at home isn't very nice. There's lots of shouting from mum and dad just seems to take no notice...!'*

Nullah looking down at the lock on his bike, doesn't say anything, he gently kicks the tyre of the bike wheel and continues attending to his bike and then putting his backpack onto his back. He goes to walk off, turns to Nick, and says, *'I'll see you after school; are you still coming to Aunty Betty's?'* Nick replies, *'Of course I am, I'll see you then!'*

Chapter Five
Meeting with Aunty Betty

Mrs Zayed was back in the classroom, and ready for her next class. She reminds the students of the two new images, and her paper handouts she gave out at the end of the last lesson. She says, '...*please get the images out and we will speak about them!*'

By showing the images, she reminds her class of their last lesson. Most of the students have the handouts, but some were away from school that day, so they were not given their worksheets or handouts, and now the class wait while these students receive their lesson information!

She then says, *'before we speak about these two images, I want to introduce you to another hormone, and that is cortisol and fits nicely with adrenalin.'*

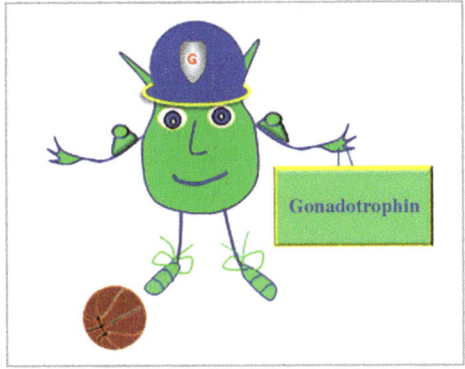

Some of the children had heard of cortisol but some had not! With this, Jai is asked by Mrs Zayed, *'please*

hand these out Jai, and we will start the lesson!' Jai does as he is asked.

She continues, '...when we are stressed, not only do we experience the 'adrenaline rush', but we can also release cortisol, so what is cortisol?' She makes and states the statement combined with the question!

Mrs Zayed did not expect the children to know, but Nick puts his hand up with an answer. Mrs Zayed, says to Nick, 'Would you like to tell the class?'

Nick stands and takes a quick gulp of air. As he was still new at the school, not many children knew him, so this, he felt, was a very brave move on his part! He begins to tell the class what he knows about cortisol, '...well, I know it is called a stress hormone which helps my body change when I'm frightened, I know that cortisol carries different messages to different parts of my body.' He stops talking and takes another deep breath, and begins again, '...so if I'm frightened, this hormone sends a message to my legs to move faster, so then I run out of danger!'

Mrs Zayed is impressed by his answer, and replies, *'You must be interested in this topic Nick,'* Nick replies, as he sits back down on his chair, *'Yes, Miss, I am!'*

Mrs Zayed now wants to speak about how cortisol and adrenalin work together. She brings the two images back up onto the screen.

She begins to speak, and says, *'...each day, cortisol, has several roles or jobs it does to keep your body healthy. It helps to regulate your blood pressure, that is how fast or slow your blood is moving around your body, it also helps you to learn and form new memories that are stored in your brain; it helps you to digest your food and manages how your body works to separate the protein, fat, or carbohydrate in the food you eat. So, it is not only a stress hormone, but it is an important hormone that helps your body to stay healthy.'*

One girl in the class, puts her hand up to speak, and Mrs Zayed, points to her, and says, *'Mani, did you want* to say something?' Mani, replies, '...Yes Miss, by brother is a diabetic and he was told that cortisol also helps in regulating our blood sugar. So, if we eat sugary and processed food our body needs more insulin released but it also needs cortisol, is that true, Miss?'

Mrs Zayed is very impressed with the responses she is getting from her class, she then replies, 'I believe it is and thank you for your informative answer, Mani.'

Inquisitive about the conversation that is going on in the classroom, Nullah, then puts up his hand to ask a question. Mrs Zayed, points to Nullah and says, '...would you like to say something Nullah?' Nullah, stands, and replies, '...yes, Miss, I just have one question, you were speaking about, protein, fat, and carbohydrate, what is carbohydrate, Miss?'

Mrs Zayed is very impressed by the students and the intelligent questions they are asking. Mrs Zayed then replies, 'I'm so glad you have asked that question Nullah and thank you for asking it.' She continues, '...there are two types of carbohydrate, one, is complex carbohydrate such as eating an apple or a slice of whole grain bread; these are good carbohydrates, and your body likes these. The other is processed carbohydrate which is found in all processed food such as doughnuts, processed and takeaway food, many ice creams, and many other foods; your body does not like these! You may like the taste in your mouth, but your body will eventually reject these carbohydrates by making you sick, overweight or with some other illness!'

Mrs Zayed wants to move on to speak about adrenalin and its role in the human body. Because her students are showing such interest in the subject, they all become energised and want to know more, but Mrs Zayed is aware of the time and must keep the group moving forward.

She makes a statement, *'adrenaline is also a hormone, and many hormones can make us act differently, they can make our behaviour change...!'* Before Mrs Zayed could say another word, one boy in the class, rudely interrupts Mrs Zayed!

Mrs Zayed, asks him, *'...would you like to add something to this conversation?'* He replied, *'I don't believe that hormones can affect your behaviour, Miss, because it doesn't make sense....!'* Mrs Zayed politely replied, *'...that is fine to have an opinion, but we will move on with the instruction as we have a lot of information to talk about and perhaps, as we go through the lessons, you will see how some hormones work differently...!'*

After the interruption, Mrs Zayed continued, *'...when we have a lot of adrenalin in our body, we are either rushing to catch a bus, or have just been accused of doing something we didn't do, or somebody wants to have an argument or pick a fight! With these times, we* can feel helpless, but adrenaline still flows through our body because we start to get mad, annoyed, angry, or frustrated! It is with these feelings that adrenaline is released. Adrenaline also helps us to run from danger and helps to keep us safe!' She takes a pause, '...when adrenaline continues to be released and we don't control the feelings of anger or hurt we have, this is when cortisol may be released within our body. If this is so, the two out of control hormones, adrenaline and cortisol can lead to us feeling anxious, nervous, frustrated and eventually make us sick. That is not a good outcome!'

She then asks, '...are there any more questions on those hormones?' The class sit in complete silence, they are all clearly still thinking about the teacher's last spoken sentences. She continues, 'We have previously spoken about adrenaline and cortisol, but most things that work in life have balance! To keep your body and brain balanced, it is good to do sport, have hobbies, or do the good things you like doing; these can help to keep your body's system balanced. When you enjoy the things you do, your body and brain are happy...!' She then puts another image up on the screen. She takes a moment to look at the students. The rude boy then says, 'That's a different colour to the other cortisol we saw....!' Mrs Zayed, replies, '...excellent, you can see *the colours and his face are happier, that is because he is not feeling so stressed, angry, or frustrated, this is because there is less cortisol going around in the body!'*

With Mrs Zayed's comment, the boy stands up and takes a bow to the other students. Mrs Zayed waits patiently for the class to settle which they do very quickly.

Mrs Zayed wants to move on as the time is running by and with the students taking 'such interest in the subject', she thinks…!

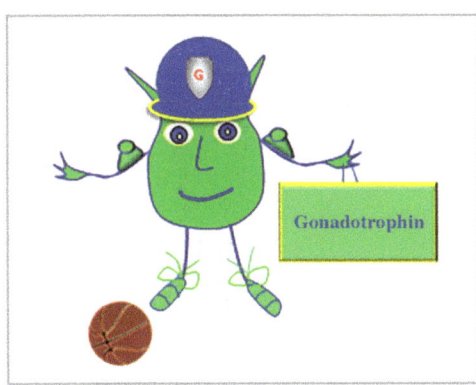

With the class now settled, she continues, *'the next handout you were given was gonadotropin; this hormone is essential for normal growth, sexual development, and reproduction. Not all hormones work on their own, many are produced to support other hormones.*

Gonadotropin is stimulated by other hormones which are stimulated by the pituitary gland.

Do you remember class, we did that exercise earlier to find out where the pituitary gland sits in your brain?'

She shows the previously shown image of the human brain on the screen and continues, *'Gonadotropins have a main function and that is to work with the gonads, meaning, the gonad is the sex or reproductive gland in both females and males. The female reproductive cell are egg cells, and in males, the reproductive cells are sperm!'*

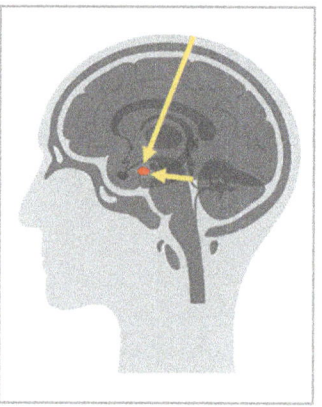

Mrs Zayed waited for any questions or misbehaving from her class, but they were there, waiting for more information...!

With Mrs Zayed's last comment, the school bell rings and the learning for the school day has finished.

As planned, Nick and Nullah rode their bikes to Aunty Betty's house where she is waiting!

She saw that Jai wasn't with them and asked why? Nullah told her, '...*he is explaining his schoolwork on hormones to his dad; they have agreed to talk the subject through!'*

Aunty Betty listened to Nullah and then replied, '...*that's very good, more parents and grandparents need to take an interest in this subject, after all, we were all children once and we have all been on this journey, I honestly don't know why people hide it away, don't talk about it or pretend it isn't happening. It makes no sense at all!*'

The next thing she asks, '*Nullah did you bring your book with you?*' Both Nullah and Nick produce their exercise books and Aunty Betty starts to tell them more about hormones.

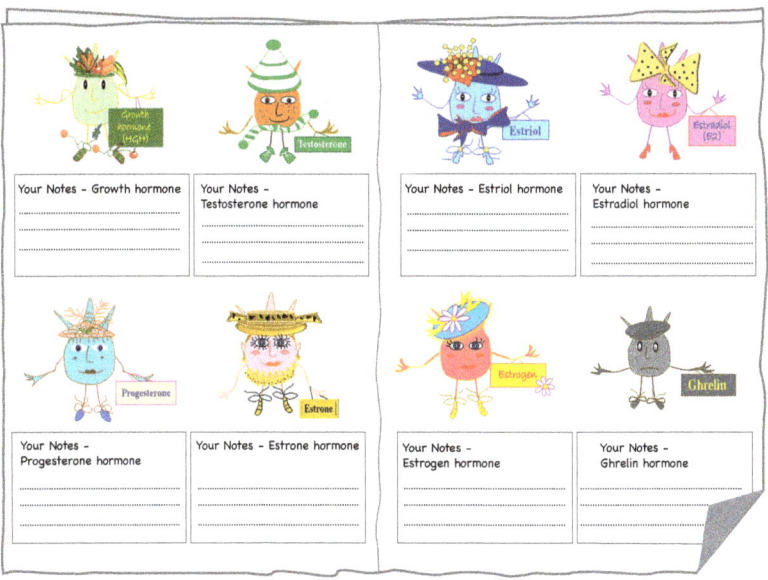

She says, '*Yesterday we got to the hormone, testosterone; do you have any questions about the hormones we have spoken about so far?*'

Nullah and Nick looked at each other, and both replied *'No'*. Aunty Betty was wiser than that, she knew that as the boys grew older, they would have many more questions...! She nods her head in reply, looks at the boys faces and both Nick and Nullah knew there were many more questions in the future!

With the workbooks open, the next hormone to speak about was progesterone.

Aunty Betty started with the question, *'What did your teacher tell you about progesterone?'* Blushing, Nullah replied, *'...we were told that progesterone is high in girls when they are ready to make a baby!'*

Aunty Betty nods her head in answer, she then says, *'...progesterone is important to the body. Low progesterone may be responsible for headaches, gaining weight and mood swings and other feelings of not feeling well.'*

She continues, *'boys and men make progesterone in their bodies, they need this hormone to balance the testosterone their body makes!'*

Aunty Betty, asks, *'are there any questions on this hormone?'*

Aware of the time, Nick looks at his watch and realises he has only about fifteen minutes left to speak with Aunty Betty and to hear her answers to their questions.

Aunty Betty, is a sensitive woman, she realises that the boys are running out of time and says, *'OK, let's have a look at those sheets your teacher gave you last week….!'*

The boys look into their school bags and pull out two crumpled sheets. One was adrenaline and the other gonadotropin.

Aunty Betty looked at both sheets and replied, *'I'm glad you are being made aware of these hormones, they are very important for your body and your good health!'*

Aunty Betty looks at the two boys as she waits to start speaking about the next hormone, while the crumpled sheets sit on the kitchen bench.

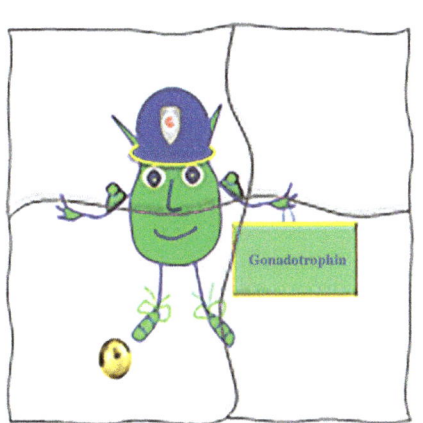

She takes a minute to look at the hormones on the bench, and says, 'it's rather interesting to see hormones in this way…!'

Nick, again, looks at his watch, and quickly remarks, *'…cricks, I* need to rush, I've got to pick up some groceries for mum and the shop will soon be closed!' With this, Nick grabs his school bag from the floor, says his *'goodbye'* and jumps on his bike to get to the shop in time before it closes!

Once Nick had left Aunty Betty's, she said to Nullah, *'I'm coming to your school next week to speak to your year about hormones. Mrs Zayed and I will be speaking, and we will discuss so many more hormones than we've spoken about so far!'* She takes a moment to show Nullah the handouts she was preparing!

As Aunty Betty lays the sheets on the bench, she says, '…serotonin, and *dopamine*, in the right amounts in your body, help endorphins and become happy hormones!'

Nullah looks at the images, he then points his finger to the bright pink image and thinks, 'I do feel happy just looking at this…'

He then looks at the sad image. Aunty Betty then

says, '...Nullah, can you feel the difference in yourself when you just look at these images...?'

Nullah, had to admit to his Aunty, 'Yes, I do! Why is this?'

She replied, '...we are all very sensitive, and everything that we experience influences our senses. Therefore, cold winter days can make us unhappy and depressed! And sometimes, things that happen in our life can also make us feel this way!'

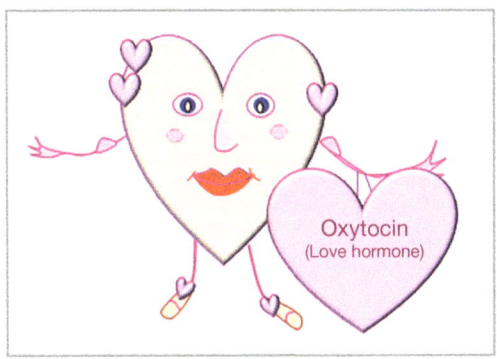

Nullah takes a minute to look at the next image his Aunty had put on the kitchen bench.

He looks at his aunt, and asks, 'what is oxytocin Aunty?'

She replies, '...this is an interesting hormone because most people fall in love at some time in their life! And many times, we can be in love with someone, but they don't love us back and that can hurt us, but we may still be in love with that person! If this happens, we release oxytocin!

Because love is an emotion, and human beings work all day and every day with their emotions, and some days, we see or find someone, and fall in love. This feeling of *love is released by oxytocin, or the Love Hormone as it is called!'*

Realising the time, Aunty Betty wants to squeeze another image of a hormone in before Nullah leaves.

She quickly says, *'and Nullah, I will quickly tell you about dopamine….'* Nullah replies, *'Aunty, you mean there are more hormones….!'* Aunty Betty looks at her nephew and replies, *'Yes, Nullah, there are over fifty….!'* She waits for Nullah's reply, he didn't reply, he was speechless. She continues, *'And each hormone is a messenger in your body, it sends and takes messages to and from your brain and other parts of your body….!*

She shows him the next handout!

He takes a moment to look at the image looking back at him, and says, *'Wow', this looks like a good time hormone,'* and asks, *'Is this a party hormone Aunty?'*

She takes her time to reply, *'this hormone helps you to have regular sleep, in your learning and concentration and how you use your body, for example, when you run or are in a race! It can however be a very demanding hormone...!'* Nullah looks at his Aunty and asks, *'...what do you mean by demanding?'* She replies, *'We hear a lot about alcohol and people taking illegal drugs, vaping, smoking, we also hear about people wanting to eat larger quantities of take away food than their body needs, fizzy drinks, after eating, drinking, or taking something that makes the brain feel good, it becomes an addiction; they become addicted to feeling good!*

This feeling good, has become a habit and so the brain wants more and more of either narcotic substances, unhealthy food and drink or something that is not good for the brain and body. Dopamine, when kept in control is very good for the brain and body, but if it becomes out of control through addiction, it is very difficult to break the addiction!'

'However,' Nullah, now knew a stern message was going to be said, *'...if you take or do any of the above, for instance, vaping, drugs, alcohol, and the other poisons I have mentioned, your body also releases dopamine!*

When your body demands more of anything that is not normal to you, this is when you develop bad habits and bad habits make your brain and body suffer and make you sick!

Nullah looked at the clock above the kitchen stove, and it was much later than he and his aunt had realised. When Aunty Betty sees the shock on Nullah's face, she says, *'Don't worry Nullah, I'm going to drive you home; you can put your bike in the back of the truck, and I'll drop you off on my way to the women's meeting!'*

Chapter Six
The rites of passage into Manhood

It was Friday afternoon, and on the way home from school, the baker at the 'hot bread' shop called to the three boys, '...are you boys interested in some part-time work on a Saturday and Sunday morning?' The baker waits for a sign to tell him the boys were interested! Each boy stops to speak to the baker, and the baker explains, '...it means sweeping the floors, cleaning sinks, making sure the windows are clean before we open the shop in time for our customers? If you are interested, be here at seven o'clock in the morning, and we'll get you started...!'

The three agreed, they would like some work and would talk to their parents that night!

The three, when getting home, each asked their parents if they could do a few hours of work for the baker on a Saturday and Sunday mornings at the 'hot bread' shop, and all parents agreed!

It's Saturday morning and the boys meet precisely at seven, they meet the baker as he had said, and each boy had his set job to do. 'It all must be spic-n-span by nine because that's when the first customers will come in the door, are you all OK with that?' said the baker!

Each got on with their jobs, Nick, was cleaning out the crumbs and baked-on ingredients from the ovens, Nullah had to clean inside the display windows where the fresh cakes and bread would be displayed, and Jai was cleaning tables and floors and putting out the rubbish into secure food rubbish bins.

They each worked for their two hours, the baker paid them, and they rode their bikes to the park to take a rest!

Nick, resting on his bike, said to the other two boys, *'that was a lot of work, but it feels good to have been paid for the work I did...!'* The three agreed and continued to eat the freshly made pies the baker had given them for breakfast!

With their breakfast over, each boy made his way home to do the jobs their mums and dads had told them to do. Nullah was helping with tidying his room, Jai was going to help his mum with the shopping before his relatives arrived and Nick thought he might do some more reading about hormones. They each agreed to meet in the park a bit later that day and then go for a ride up the mountain!

They meet as planned and rode their bikes up the mountain paths seeing different wildlife, sometimes stopping to speak about the Australian bush and sometimes just to chat about the future plans they each had...!

With the weekend over, and well into the next week of school and the night that most kids dread, Parent – Teacher Nights where the students went along with their parents to hear about, not only their child's academic achievements, but the social, and positive contributions they have put into their school and community.

Like so many different buildings, schools too, have their own unique feeling, and character. This is the character that children become use to. If a school is pleasant and friendly, this comes through in the feelings that are received by the child's parents' as they walk into and through the front door.

Jai's dad made a point of saying, *'This is a nice school, and it makes me feel so good Jai, that you are coming to this school for your education.'* Jai too, liked his school and knew that he was lucky to be safe and going to school in such a nice place.

Jai, his mum, and dad bumped into Nullah, his mum and dad, in the school corridor. The families greeted one another and were happy to see each other. Once the greetings were over, Jai, and his parents continued to walk into the waiting room, (one of Jai's old classroom's). Just leaving, he met Nick with his mum and dad; they were on their way out of the classroom as Jai and his parents walked in through the classroom door. Jai said, *'Hi'* to Nick and his parents. Nick, then introduced his mum and dad to Jai, and Jai's mum and dad. Jai, couldn't help thinking to himself, 'Nick, looks relieved that his mum and dad have met my mum and dad!'

Jai's dad wanted to know more about Nick, he asked, *'Is that one of your friends Jai?'* Jai replied with a simple, *'Yes'*.

From the teachers' reports, Jai was doing well at school and both his mum and dad made a point of telling their son how proud they were of him. His mum, while they were walking out of the school building, was saying, *'it would be nice to have Nullah and his family around for lunch on Sunday!'* She then said, *'What do you think about that Jai?'*

Jai's dad quickly says, and before Jai could make a comment, *'I think that would be a good idea, once the new baby arrives, we will be busy, and for a few months, we will not have any time for entertaining!'*

Jai, nods his head, and then says, *'I think that would be a great idea.'* He then continues, *'...do you think we can ask Nick and his mum and dad, also?'* His mum replies, *'that would be nice, yes, ask them too!'*

As they walk out of the building and into the school grounds, the sun is setting behind some night encroaching clouds, the air is still, and the birds are sending out their last calls for the day! Jai's dad, 'stops in is tracks', puts his hands on his hips, sniffs the air and says, *'A perfect end to a perfect day.'*

With that, he puts his arms around his wife and son as they walk along the pathway to their home.

Before Sunday arrives, Nullah knows that Aunty Betty is coming to the school to give a talk with Mrs Zayed! 'That day is quickly coming closer!' He thinks!

The day arrives, and the whole of Jai's, Nullah's and Nick' Year is gathered in the Assembly Hall! All the students were having the same instruction, so each had learnt about many hormones, what they hadn't learnt was the new hormones they are about to be shown!

With their workbooks open, the lesson begins.

Both Aunty Betty and Mrs Zayed, are ready to speak to the students; Mrs Zayed starts the conversation. During her introduction, she asks the students to interact with herself, and Aunty Betty, she explains, *'After you see each slide, we will have a short talk about what*

we know about each hormone. First, I want to speak about reducing your "adrenaline rush". Many students suffer with nerves as the exams come around, but when you know how to work with your body and brain, you not only become in control, but you also become the owner of your own body, brain, and mind!' She stops, asks, *'Are there any questions about this slide?'* There were no questions, so she continues.

On invitation, Aunty Betty now steps forward to speak to the group. She says, '*...do you remember, one of the last hormones Mrs Zayed spoke about was oxytocin, of course there are so many more hormones in your body than we have time to tell you about here at school!'*

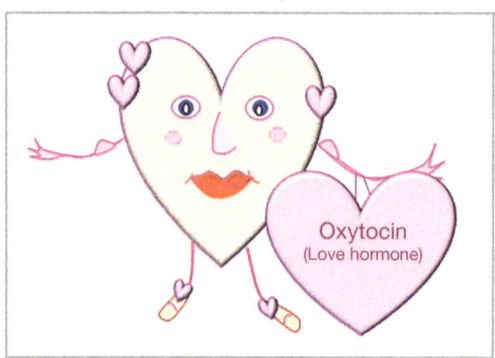

She stops, takes a breath, and continues, '*Our body is made of human and sensitive technology. We are not always aware of the body language our body is sending out in different messages. For instance, when we fall in love, our lips can become redder than is usual! Our body makes these adjustments without any known signal from us! Feelings and hormones can be deceptive! We can feel happy and think we are madly in love, when, in fact, it can be infatuation!*

Often love, can turn to anger and this is when, oxytocin is thought to go from a high to a low!'

'When we start to learn about hormones and how they work in our body, we can become aware of the feelings or emotions we experience. When people say and feel 'green with envy', this could be the reversal of the role oxytocin plays in their body, when in fact, they could be jealous or angry with someone and the 'once felt love' turns to anger and frustration. These feelings or reactions may lead to a low release of oxytocin!

Understanding these hormone differences, is all about growing up and becoming responsible adults. As your body changes, different hormones will start to do their job, females will change differently to males!

The female's brain is different to a male's brain and therefore each person's perception of different events they experience, will be different, and hormones play a big role in individual perception!'

She continues, *'The next hormone I want to speak to you about is melatonin. Melatonin is the hormone that helps you to sleep. During puberty, many of you will experience restless nights and possibly, not sleep. This* is due to how your body is reacting and a possible reduction in melatonin!

Science is not sure why this happens at puberty and more research is ongoing!'

She stops, looks at her audience to see the reaction, and then continues, *'Because of this restlessness, many young people play on devices late into the night and early morning. By doing this, the brain becomes over stimulated and if melatonin is low, the chances of having a good night's rest is difficult to achieve!*

So, what is the solution? Turn all devices off at least an hour before bed. Go for a walk, play a ball game in the yard or garden, do some deep breathing and relaxation exercises!'

The students were attentive when Aunty Betty put the next slide on the screen.

Aunty Betty looks at the group of young faces looking back at her, and then says, '...this hormone helps you to have regular sleep, in your learning and concentration and how you use your body, for example, when you run; it can, however, be a very demanding hormone...!'

'Dopamine is needed to keep you healthy and well.' She pauses, and then starts again, 'Dopamine, may be called "The Party Hormone" because it likes to party and if too much is released into your body through, either vaping, alcohol, illegal drug taking, gambling, overeating too much junk or unhealthy food, or drinking too much fizzy drink and other harmful behaviours to your body, your brain will demand more! Once a bad habit is established your brain's demands will increase...!'

When you exercise and feel great after any sports event, you have a little dopamine released, this makes you feel good.'

She stops her talk, pauses, looks at the students, then continues, *'You need just enough dopamine to keep you healthy and working to your capacity!'*

She continues, *'By eating a healthy diet full of whole food, you can help with keeping your dopamine levels healthy. Foods such as, beef, chicken, almonds, eggs, avocados, and bananas all help with keeping your brain healthy and this allows you to stay motivated, assists with learning new concepts, allows you to compete at sporting events and generally allows you to feel good which helps you to maintain your good health!'*

However, when your dopamine levels are interfered with through, she repeats her message," *...vaping, smoking, alcohol consumption, eating too much junk food, drug taking, then you need to recall the messages you are learning in this session!"'*

Aunty Betty takes a moment to look at the group, then continues with her talk, *'as we all know, there are boys and girls, or males and females, and there is a very good reason for this, it is to allow for survival of the species!*

When a male, goes into puberty, his body changes from a boy to a man, it is the activation of many of your hormones that takes you on this journey, both into and through puberty...!'

She pauses, then continues and mentions her Aboriginal connections, '*This in Aboriginal culture is a very special time for young males.*' Nullah, feels a little embarrassed, but soon realises, how proud he is of his ancestry, and thinks, 'That's great to hear from Aunty Betty!' Aunty Betty continues, '*...men usually grow more hair than women, they have stronger muscles this allows them to do heavy manual work!*'

The group sat quietly as Aunty Betty gave her talk. She now introduces two more slides, the first of which, many of the students had seen before. She notices, the group wriggle a little in their seats as they look at the slides. She continues, '*The main use of the penis is to wee or excrete wastewater. At puberty, the penis is also used to release sperm! So how does a penis release sperm?*' She asks the question, not expecting an answer, so continues, '*To allow this to happen, the penis needs to be in an erection. The penis shaft fills with blood and this is what makes the penis stiff. An erection is not dirty or naughty, it is a natural body process to keep the penis healthy. An erection can be an involuntary action, meaning the penis becomes erect because it is a natural body response! An erection can also be brought on by different thoughts or by stimulation!*

So, what is sperm?' *Sperm is the smallest human cell. Each male makes many thousands of sperm every second, so there are a lot of sperm produced. In this slide you can see the testicles and penis. There is nothing new or mysterious about the way the human body is made. It is indeed, a superbly developed design in human technology! So, let's look at how the male body works,'* she says.

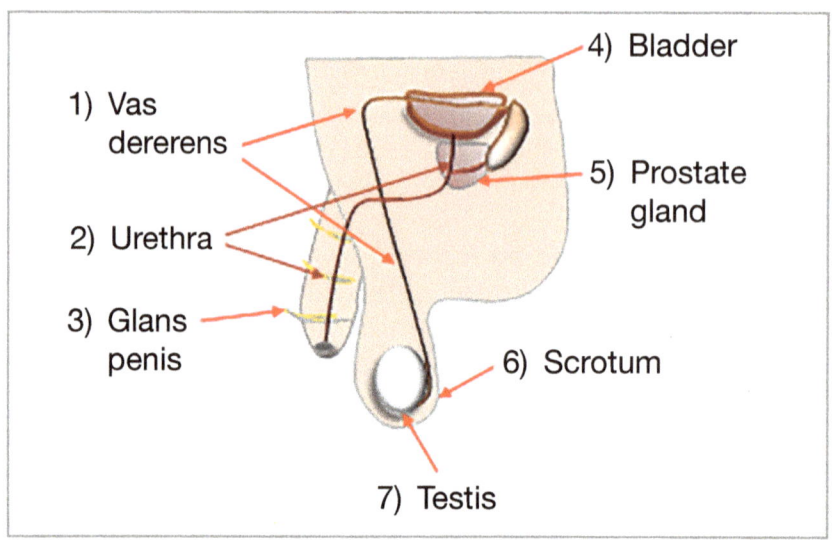

'First, number 1) the Vas deferens, is the tube that carries the sperm from the testes, number 7). 2) is the urethra, this is the tube that carries your wee or urine; it is the waste from the fluids you drink. 3) is the penis and known as a glans or member. 4) is your bladder and is where your wee or urine is stored. You know when you need to release urine because you get a twinge or message in your brain, 'you need to go to the bathroom!' 5) is the prostate gland and this regulates sperm, when it travels up the vas deferens to the prostate gland, number 5). By the time the sperm reaches the prostate gland, it becomes tired. The prostate supplies much needed energy for the sperm to carry on its journey. The energy is supplied to the sperm in carbohydrate, we previously spoke about

carbohydrate, do you remember?' Some of the students, nod their heads as Aunty Betty, looks at the different responses she gets! She then continues, *'Once the sperm passes through the prostate, the sperm continues its journey and leaves the penis through ejaculation!' This is when the penis is in erection!* She stops, then looks at the class and continues, *'6) is the scrotum, as a male enters puberty, the scrotum, like the penis, grows, it might also go darker in colour. The scrotum has the role and is loose in the summer heat but will tighten up when the body gets cold.'* She explains, *'the scrotum is involuntary, and works by itself protecting the sperm and testes at all times, through either extreme heat or cold!'* she then asks, *'...are there any questions?'*

Without a reply, she continues, *'Now, let's look at the journey of a sperm! Please always remember, the way your body works, is the way it keeps you healthy and well.'*

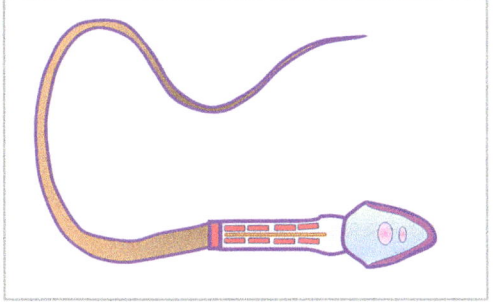

She continues, *'Sperm are made in the testes, number seven on your sheet, and many thousand are made with every heartbeat during the day and while a male sleeps!'* Once mature, the sperm travel up the Vas deferens, number one, on your sheet, and eventually come to the prostate gland. Now, the prostate gland is an important part of the male body because, Aunty Betty takes a breath, and continues, *'the prostate gland is about the size of a walnut and is responsible for making the seminal fluid in semen, semen is a cloudy to white sticky fluid, and supplies the energy to the sperm that propels it forward in an ejaculation!'*

She takes a pause, and then says, *'...are there any questions?'* The students sit quietly in their seats, then one boy says, *'Miss Betty, if there are many thousands of sperm made all the time, whether we are asleep or awake, do all the sperm leave in one ejaculation?'*

Aunty Betty replies. *'...what a good question, thank you for that.'* She thinks, then says, *'Not all sperm are healthy sperm, some die before leaving the testes, if so, the chemicals which make the sperm are absorbed back into the body, some sperm die early, and while on the journey; it is the healthiest sperm that survive. As the body is continually making sperm, I would think, there are always new sperm to replace the old or dead sperm...!*

She starts her talk again, *'so, now let's look at the journey of the sperm...!'*

She takes a breath, and then says, *'...before the sperm starts its journey, it may be stored in the testes!*

The sperm travels up the Vas deferens, collects the seminal fluid needed for the rest of the journey, then travels along the urethra to be released at the end of the penis. The function of ejaculation helps to keep the penis clean and sperm healthy!'

She takes a pause, and swallows deeply, then continues her talk.

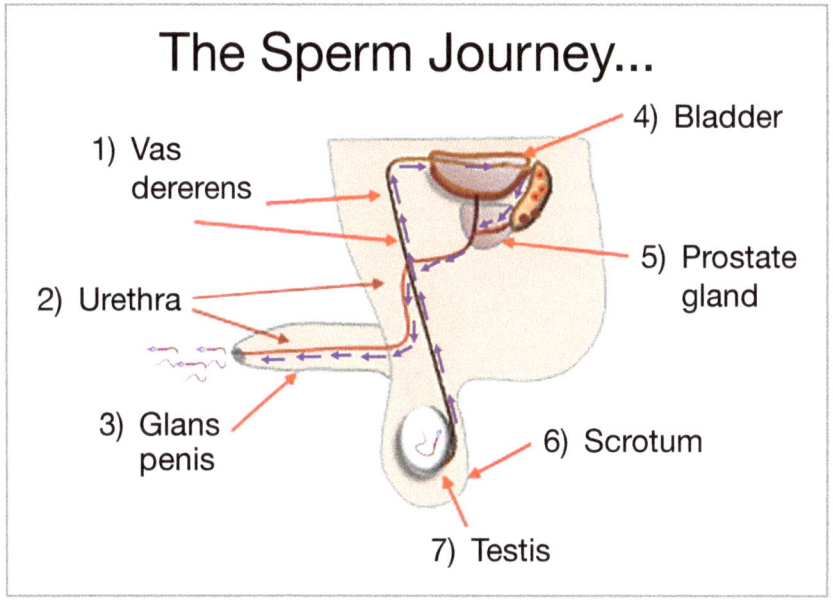

'Sperm always takes priority over urine or wee and will be released before wee!'

She waits for any comments then speaks again, *'...sperm is not just a wet and sticky substance, it contains great amounts of information, which include the acrosome, mitochondria, and the nucleus, it also carries other information, but we will only speak of the three just mentioned. The acrosome carries enzymes* which allow it to penetrate the female egg, the nucleus is the direct head of the sperm, and it is this head that works within the female egg once fertilisation takes place! The mitochondria are seen on the slide,' she takes a breath and continues, '...mitochondria contain a mixture of proteins and enzymes and your DNA. Of course, a sperm carries more information than that, it is also made up of organic molecules!'

She stops, pauses, and then says, '...are there any questions, we have covered a lot of information so far and we are nearly at the end of the talk?'

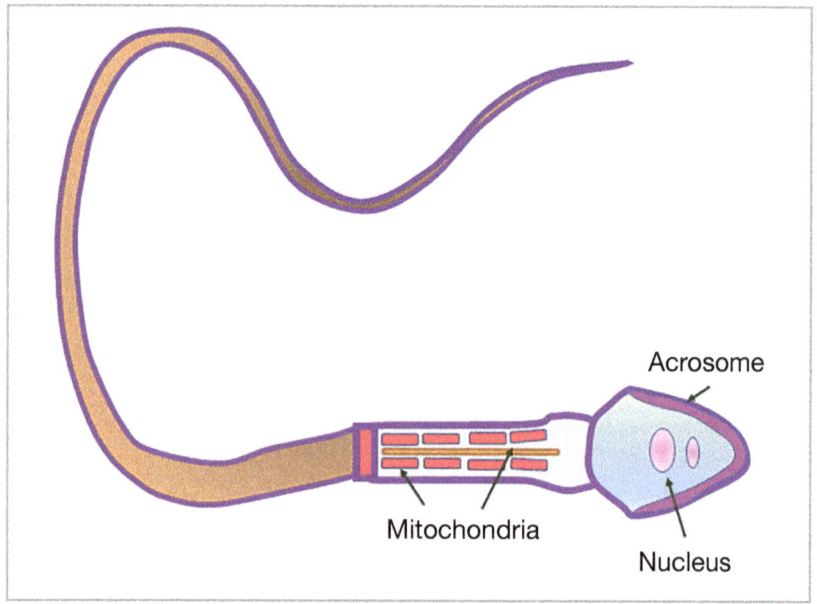

Then one student puts up their hand and asks, 'What is a molecule, Miss?' Aunty Betty replies and says, 'Thank you, that is an important question; molecules vary in *different sizes and a protein molecule is the largest. On average, there are one hundred million in every 25mm or one square inch. How I like to describe molecules, if you eat a 25mm or one inch of a fresh banana, you will be eating the equivalent of one hundred million molecules; there are good molecules and altered molecules, but that is yet another subject. Molecules are found in the air you breathe, the food you eat, including junk food, this food is not always made up of good molecules, so you should be aware and think, is this food good for me to eat and then think about the molecules within it?'*

She was now running out of time, and apologises, saying, *'...because the mitochondria have so much information and we have covered only some of this information in our topic on puberty, we will need to have the molecule debate another time!'*

Close to the end of the talk, Aunty Betty says, *'with my closing words, I want to say',* She pauses, then says to the students, *'A female body is made differently to a male body and this is with good purpose, it is to create the next generation of people just like yourselves, by doing this, it ensures the future of the species, but...',* she pauses, *'if in the act of sexual intercourse, respect for each other is lost, it can cause hurt, pain, humiliation, and sadness!'*

Mrs Zayed, nods her head in agreement, then says to Aunty Betty, *'Thank you so much for an informative afternoon, I'm sure we will have many more questions in the future...!'*

With the school day over, Nullah, Jai and Nick meet at the bike shed where they look at their notes and talk about the lesson with Aunty Betty. It was now time to head home for dinner.

Part Two
WORKING TOGETHER
For young adults and their family

RESPECT

POINTS FOR TALKING ABOUT

1. The flexible nature of Jai and Nullah's good relationship, how does this benefit both boys?
   ....
   ....
   ....
   ....

2. Respect for Nick is shown when he joins the established relationship of Nullah and Jai, how would you accept another person joining yourself and your friend?
   ....
   ....
   ....
   ....

3. Nullah is a First Nation Australian, because both Jai and Nick want to learn about the Australian bush; they show confidence in the information that Nullah tells them, especially when it comes to keeping them safe when a large brown snake comes very close to them while they are in the bush. How can you add to their story?
   ....
   ....
   ....
   ....

4. Nick does not seem to have a friendly family like Jai and Nullah, if this happens to a friend of yours, what can you do to help your friend?

   ....
   ....
   ....
   ....

5. During the story, Jai learns his mum is pregnant, and he can expect either, a new brother or sister in the coming months; do you think Jai wants to know more about this future sibling?

   ....
   ....
   ....
   ....

6. Aunty Betty is a wiser, older First Nation lady; she is a qualified doctor, a GP, and encourages the boys to learn more about not only hormones but what else is she teaching them?

   ....
   ....
   ....

7. Would you say that care, respect, honesty, and trust came through with the story?

   Your answer and discussion:

   ....
   ....
   ....
   ....
   ....

8. During the story, Jai and his dad takes some quality time out to learn from each other and to enjoy the moment, how can you do this with either a brother, sister, mum, dad, aunty, uncle, grandparent, or friend? Please think carefully, write your answer down and then, act and do the response you have written about.

   ....
   ....
   ....
   ....
   ....
   ....
   ....

YOUR NOTES

**Part Three
WORKING TOGETHER
For young adults and their family**

OPENING UP THE CONVERSATION

CONTINUING THE JOURNEY

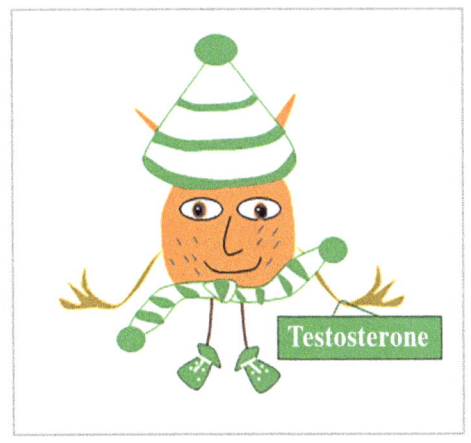

Testosterone is needed for the development of male sex organs. During the mother's pregnancy, testosterone helps in the development of the penis and testes in the unborn child.

During puberty, testosterone helps in the growth of hair in the armpit, around and within the pubic area; it promotes the deepening of the male voice; the development of muscle mass, and strength, and works in the manufacture of sperm production. Other benefits of testosterone; it aids in bone strength and helps to fight bone disorders, possibly later in life, such as osteoporosis. Testosterone plays a key role in both males and females.

The hormone Gonadotropin's main function is to help to control the functions within the ovaries and testes. Gonadotropins are important for the regulation and proper functioning related to male and female reproduction.

Gonadotropins are made in the pituitary gland in response to other hormone stimulation in the hypothalamus. The process is carried out by the hypothalamus pituitary gonad axis.

Having an 'adrenaline rush' is great to get you out of danger, but too much adrenaline can make you stressed, and easily upset. In the older male, he might turn to smoking, alcohol, gambling, or drug abuse to take a break from the nervous reactions he's experiencing. In younger males, they may try vaping, drug taking, alcohol or other forms of narcotics. Take control of the situation by playing sport, doing relaxation exercises and yoga; all will help to reduce too much adrenaline.

Too much cortisol in your body's system is like too much adrenaline. Take control. If you find you are using destructive substances to keep your nervous reaction in place. STOP, take a breath, and rethink the damage substances can do to your health, behaviour, relationships, and wellbeing. Remember, you are in charge, not the substances!

The serotonin hormone helps to regulate the brain to normalise certain emotions. It carries messages by transmitting between nerve cells in the brain and to other parts of the body. It is known to regulate mood, digestion, sleep, nausea and breathing. It may act as an anti-depressant through different emotional states or mood swings. Too much serotonin and too little serotonin can lead to different health conditions or outcomes.

Reduced serotonin may be due to a health condition and should be managed by a professional health practitioner.

It may lead to depression, anxiety, impulsive behaviour, and sleepless nights.

Oxytocin is known as the 'love hormone', but it has other functions! It is linked to your feelings of empathy, trust, group memories, social bonding, and recognition.

Oxytocin is produced in the hypothalamus, then transported to the pituitary gland at the base of the brain. In females, it helps during childbirth and breastfeeding.

Low oxytocin levels may be connected to depression, anxiety, or mood swings. Oxytocin levels can vary depending on life experiences, lifestyle, and the food you eat.

Always seek professional and medical advice if you have concerns.

Melatonin is made in the pineal gland, a small pea-sized gland, found in the middle of the human mid-brain in the brain.

It works as a stimulant to the body and tells us when to sleep or when to wake up! This hormone works in response to darkness.

The hormone works with your body clock and the forces of night and day. Once evening starts to descend, your body clock kicks in, and you will start to feel sleepy. Melatonin levels, in healthy people are elevated for around twelve hours, allowing people to have a good night's sleep!

Melatonin has many roles, it regulates your sleep cycle; in females, it plays a role in the menstruation cycle. Research is showing that young people, during puberty, may have low melatonin levels.

In reduced melatonin levels, it may cause mood swings, disruption in sleep pattens and other health conditions.

Like all hormonal levels, each needs to be balanced in your body. By eating a balanced diet that is rich in fruit, vegetables, nuts, including bananas, berries, cherries, oranges, pineapple, corn, asparagus, tomatoes, olives, broccoli, peanuts, sunflower seeds, flaxseed, and mustard seeds. Also include in your diet, protein, including, chicken, eggs, fish, cheese and some whole grain, complex carbohydrate, such as whole grain breads. All these foods help to increase your melatonin level.

Like so many hormones, dopamine is made in your brain. It is important, again, to have the right amount of dopamine, this keeps your thinking and behaviour balanced. Dopamine has a role in controlling your moods, memory, sleep, concentration, learning and your body movements.

Dopamine helps the nerve cells to send messages to other parts of your brain and in the combination of group cells, it sends messages to the group. Dopamine is responsible for letting you feel pleasure, motivation, and satisfaction when you achieve something you have been aiming for; the feeling of satisfaction leads to a dopamine rush. Dopamine is responsible for the delight your experience when you eat nice food. Such delight can be induced by eating unhealthy or junk food, because your brain has registered, through past experiences, the pleasure of eating this food. Please remember, the taste buds in your mouth are connected to your brain through neuron pathways; your taste buds have nothing to do with your stomach! Your stomach will let you know when you are hungry and you need to eat, but your stomach does not tell you about what to eat, the quality or goodness of the food!

Having too much dopamine in one part of the brain, or not enough in another part of the brain, can lead to poor impulse control, some aggressive behaviour, binge eating, extreme competitiveness and other addictions.

You can produce too much dopamine in your system by creating bad habits. These habits may include drug taking, alcoholism, gambling, or by creating a craving for an unhealthy diet!

There are many signs that can suggest you have low dopamine levels, some are, continuing to feel sad or lacking in hope and little aspiration and motivation to achieve your goals. You become less excited about happy events in your life. Other signs may be muscle cramps or spasms of stiffness, digestion problems, and a lack of interest in how and why you are going into puberty!

An imbalance of dopamine or other hormones can lead to, stress, inability to sleep, drug abuse, becoming or being obese or eating too much sugar, saturated fat because of the cravings through a lack of dopamine!

Always remember, a balanced diet of whole food can keep your hormones healthy, and your body and brain balanced.

Continuing the journey

Each young male should be aware of how the lower part of his body works; this is not just the penis, but the other areas such as the scrotum, anal area and importantly, the prostate gland.

The male body has been carefully thought out and planned through nature. To treat both the male and female body with respect is the sole objective of this book.

For the penis to function properly, it needs to have erections; this keeps the penis healthy. To release sperm from the penis, is, a natural part of the male anatomy and is a natural process for the organ.

It is important for both boys and girls to become familiar with their body; to look and examine their body is a sign of responsibility. When a person knows the intimate parts of their body, they become aware of different changes that can take place in possibly the appearance of lumps, skin colour and changes and many more medical conditions that can and do happen. When this is done, unknown or unseen lumps or spots can be detected, and professional medical help or support can be quickly accessed.

When young people want privacy, it can be with good reason, after all, they are experiencing a lot of changes, not only to their physical body but to the way they think, they are becoming familiar with their brain, they may also start to behave, differently to what is expected! This is no excuse to behave badly!

Again, it is the respect shown for the human body that is paramount with gaining this knowledge.

Many young people start to ask personal questions of themselves, for instance, 'Why am I here?' 'What is my purpose?' all of which are deep, and profound questions to the young adult.

YOUR NOTES

Part Four
WORKING TOGETHER
For young adults and their family

- ✓ INVOLVEMENT
- ✓ STRUCTURE
- ✓ RECALL
- ✓ PRODUCTION AND HARVESTING

- ✓ CONSENT
- ✓ FRIENDSHIP
- ✓ COMMUNICATION
- ✓ UNDERSTANDING

YOUR BOY, BUILDING HIS SKILL BASE AND WORKING WITH HIS AMAZING BRAIN

Not all boys find learning easy, especially learning to read and write. As I have previously said, *'the boy's brain is different to a girl's brain...!'* and boys can have many difficulties in learning, what we as adults may assume as easy learning, they can find extremely difficult!

And bearing in mind, in some world societies, puberty is starting as low as seven years of age. This can put some young males well behind! Not only is their body making demands on them, but also the community in which they live! When we work exclusively with our son's there is a magic that takes place. By understanding, that boys need more nurturing at the time of puberty onset is an investment in love and caring for all concerned.

No parent should leave all education to the teachers of our children. We are equally responsible for our children's education. To sit with a child while they learn their words, or learn to read, is an investment of a lifetime, it cannot be transcended by any material gain!

INVOLVEMENT

All children learn in different ways! Some children respond well to action and movement in their learning, others like to see graphics, some like just one-on-one education, for instance, sitting down with a parent at regular times each night to hear him read or pronounce his words, works wonders in forming brain connections. The neurons can go into overdrive when your boy is learning with you sitting by his side. Showing that you care by asking questions that relate to him is also a positive way forward.

Some children have hearing problems, and this is not always detected in a busy class with large numbers of students. If your boy has been suffering with, even mild hearing loss, it will slow him down in his learning capabilities.

I can honestly say, I have never taught a dumb child or a child that cannot learn. All children have a capacity to learn, as I have said, *'...they all learn in different ways...',* and as parents or carers, it is our responsibility to find the technique that allows our boy to learn.

STRUCTURE

The human brain likes order, it does not work well when chaos is surrounding its environment! The brain's architecture and scaffolding, like structure, identity, sameness, and things to be in their rightful place!

Many children, and especially boys, suffer in their learning if there isn't a structure in place for the learning to be achieved! Each day, your boy's brain is putting down new neuron pathways and synapses that allow learning to take place. If the structure isn't there, your boy will find learning difficult to do. An important part of your boy's learning is to take responsibility for his wellbeing, this includes, from a very early age, possibly as young as five or six, to make their bed in the mornings. How they make their bed doesn't really matter, but the structure and discipline of making the bed allows new neuron pathways to be put down in the child's brain. Other simple jobs can be cleaning out the rabbit cage. If you don't have rabbits, encourage your boy, at a responsible age, to find small jobs that have payment attached, such as dog walking, looking after other people's pets while they are on holiday, other jobs may include taking on a paper run, or helping for a few hours at a local shop. All such little tasks help with building life and academic skills.

Age is not a barrier to the simple learning techniques outlined in the above; the sooner you start, the more benefits your child will gain for now and the future.

Do not fail the structure you are putting into place; if there is an interruption, for example, school holidays, travel, sickness or any other reason, the structure must be continued as soon as possible!

RECALL

Please remember, a child's brain, the pre-frontal cortex, is not completely formed until about the age of seven. So, if your boy has memory lapses or doesn't remember something, gently repeat the information. By doing this, you are reinforcing the neuron pathways that were previously put down; you are possibly filling in the blank spaces and then, 'WOW', it makes sense to him!

Even as adults, we work with our long and short-term memories and our children are no different. The one disadvantage they have, is the lack of experience to be able to 'fudge' their way through situations like us older adults!

Remembering, that the child is still putting down neuron pathways in the brain, so the new information they receive daily, is 'NEW' and not old established information that needs to be brought to the surface because of a time lapse, or a convenient dismissal of the information, which as adults, we can do!

PRODUCTION AND HARVESTING

All children have talent and ability, it is inherent in them. It is sad, when a child is considered by others to be a failure, because no child is a failure, they have just learnt in a different way and have not found the way to own their production or how to harvest their ability with the knowledge they've gained at this time in their life!

Even the simplest of 'doing' things can lead to production and harvesting. Let your boy tinker in the garage, put guidelines down, *'He Can Do This, Just So Long As He Cleans Up After He's Finished!'* The kitchen is a great place to invest in your boy's production and harvesting. Teach him how to read recipes, how to cut vegetables and not to mention, make him aware of the dangers in the kitchen.

Leggo, and what a great invention that is? But toys and children playing with them can go back many thousands of years as the spinning top found in King Tut's tomb that dates back six thousand years ago! And so it is, the more production and harvesting your boy does, the more and greater neuron pathways are put down inside his brain.

By using:

- ✓ INVOLVEMENT
- ✓ STRUCTURE
- ✓ RECALL
- ✓ PRODUCTION AND HARVESTING

Your boy will move forward in leaps and bounds. Please remember, not one of the steps above can be missed; each has a purpose and reason for being written into this book.

CONTINUING THE JOURNEY

- ✓ CONSENT
- ✓ FRIENDSHIP
- ✓ COMMUNICATION
- ✓ UNDERSTANDING

CONSENT

The age of consent for sexual activity varies, from state to state and from country to country. Having said that, each person's body belongs to no one else but themself; it is not the property of another person and should never be considered in the context of belonging to another!

Your body is your body, and you should never be coerced into giving something of yourself that you don't want to give! Emotional Blackmail is something that is not freely spoken of, but it is a system of abuse that no young male or female should experience. Such comments as:

> ➢ *'If you loved me, you would do this for me...!'*
> ➢ *'Show me you really care and let me do this to you...!'*
> ➢ *'I won't see you again if you don't let me do this...!'*
> ➢ *'If you do this, I will stay with you forever...!'*

And so, the demanding statements are made to another person, all of which should be instantly ignored. If this happens to you, remove yourself from, what has become, a toxic relationship, and you don't need this in your life.

In many relationships, there is 'implied' Emotional Blackmail, this is when the words are unspoken and the *assumption* in the relationship assumes the reaction, statement or reply from another person! Such assumptions and answers could be:

> ➢ *Assumption, 'Oh, no, they (the second person in the relationship) wouldn't like me to do that...!'*
> ➢ *Assumption, 'He/she wouldn't like me to wear that...!'*
> ➢ *Assumption, 'She won't mind if you wear her trainers...!'*

The victim in the above becomes powerless and the way forward with this situation is for the victim to voice how they feel, or if that cannot be done, is to move away and out of the coercive relationship.

For many young people learning some of the points above are difficult to do, but the knowledge of knowing how relationships work will give them an experience that will be helpful a little later in life!

FRIENDSHIP

Friendships are very precious to our young males and females. Friendship has three essential ingredients:

- ✓ CARE
- ✓ RESPECT
- ✓ TRUST

If any one of these vital points is lost in a friendship, the friendship usually doesn't survive.

When we CARE for someone, we spend special times together; we remember their birthday or a special day in their life; we let them know that we are thinking of them; we may occasionally buy them a gift because of the bond between us.

When RESPECT is in the relationship, we do not take advantage of our friend, we wait and ask our friend for their opinion, if we can use something of theirs or wait for the right opportunity to ask or speak about sensitive issues.

With TRUST, we know, if we say something to that person, it will not be repeated to other people; we trust that person with our words, precious belongings and more.

For all members of the family, friendship is about reaching out to your friend when you are having a difficult or hard time. You enjoy each other's time and company, you show you think of them by the little things you do for them; friendship has, care, respect and trust built into your relationship.

COMMUNICATION

Communication allows for understanding another person's different emotional needs or wants. Positive communication allows arguments to be settled. Positive communication allows us to interact with our friends and family and to live together. Most people have experienced arguments in the home and how tough it is to live under 'one roof' at these difficult times. Positive communication, (sitting down together and talking things through, allows people to settle their differences and end the argument or dispute).

When we positively communicate, we show we love, care and are happy to be with the people we are with. We may demonstrate this by cooking some biscuits as a surprise, doing the washing up when everybody else has walked away from the dishes in the sink! This doesn't mean you become a 'general dog's body', for everybody else! It means, you talk about the dishes in the sink, and ask, *'Whose turn is it next to do the dishes...?'* Or you might offer to help!

Communication is about giving your time to hear another's story, or to support a friend when they are going through a crisis.

Positive communication allows us to voice our honest opinion and others will give us the time to listen to our side of the story. Positive communication allows us to make changes, positive changes to the world environment where animals and people can be protected.

So, establishing the ground and making ready for positive communication has many benefits in our friendships, relationships with our families and the school and world environments.

UNDERSTANDING

As your boy grows and changes, their level of understanding will also develop into maturity. Understanding that each person has their own set of values, world beliefs and experiences takes time and learning.

We don't all see the same things in the same way. Each person will interpret different words spoken, different experiences and actions taken in different ways. It takes time to develop the 'awareness' needed to understand that we are all different.

YOUR NOTES

Part Five
WORKING TOGETHER
For young adults and their family

HYGEINE AND CARE

YOUR BOY – HIS MATURING BODY AND GROWTH SPURTS

THE BODY DEMANDS

Nature will not be told when puberty can happen to your boy. Your boy's timeclock works with his body's rhythm and will do what it needs to do when the timing is right for him and no one else!

Therefore, many teenagers, if they are not made aware of their body and the changes it will make during puberty, some outcomes can feel overwhelming or intimidating to a young male. Not only is he becoming a young man, but his body puts other demands on him; he may experience growing pains, especially when he is in bed at night! You may hear a groan or moan coming from his room, he may not even realise he is making a noise, but you hear him!

When our children sleep, their body can go into overdrive with growth spurts; it is especially seen with boys when they go a bit gangly: their feet, arms and legs all seem out of proportion. This is nature preparing them for manhood.

Not only are they growing at exponential knots, but their body, through hormone interaction, is demanding that the boy gets ready for the tasks ahead. Please also remember, your boy's brain is still maturing and will not be mature until he is about twenty-five!

Not only does he have aching joints or leg cramps, but he may suffer with skin break outs that seem almost too difficult to solve!

Understanding that fluctuating hormones may lead to the development of the skin condition, known as acne. Acne as a skin condition is related to the blood vessels in the face and other parts of the body. Acne has also been linked to the rosacea skin condition. The appearance of spots or Acne, on the face, may interfere with your boy's self-esteem and wellbeing. Many teenagers may think that acne is caused through eating too much chocolate or 'junk food', this may contribute to the condition, but it may not be the cause!

Do not use tanning beds, tanning lamps or facial scrubs to reduce the condition, this can and may exaggerate the condition.

1) Twice a day, wash with warm, clean water to remove excess dirt and oil, and
2) Use a sunscreen with a protection of 15 or higher!

Acne or rosacea conditions may be linked to simply, becoming aware 'they are growing up', self-esteem, anxiety, depression, or stress due to either academic or other 'life demands' they are experiencing.

Other areas of consideration, their body is changing - from a child to a man; this, some young males may feel is a daunting experience! Give positive encouragement and understanding and commit positive time to talk with your son.

Other areas of consideration, the body may sweat more than usual, encourage changing underwear and socks daily, especially, if he loves sport and is a keen sportsman.

Encourage daily showering, including keeping his hair clean. Use a good brand of shampoo, and body wash, possibly without sulphates! These are proving not to be good for human skin or body systems.

Your boy may experience wet dreams, this is not unusual, encourage him to change his night wear and to put clean on the following night. If possible, leave clean sheets where he can have easy access, but also let him know where to put his dirty clothes or bedding. As a parent, don't be shy, encourage him to start to do his own washing. This is not a punishment but the building of a very valuable life skill that will stay with him throughout his life.

And finally encourage him with dental hygiene keeping his teeth and gums healthy by giving his mouth daily and regular attention brushing his teeth, including gently brushing the tongue to remove any leftover residue from food and drinks. Again, these actions are all about building life skills that will stay with him for life.

YOUR NOTES

Part Six
WORKING TOGETHER
For young adults and their family

YOUR BOY HAS DREAMS

A TIME OF LEARNING AND GROWTH

ADOLESCENCE – A TIME OF ENERGY AND POSITIVE LEARNING – A TRIP TO PALESTINE

While he attended university, I can remember one of our son's going on holiday with three friends to Turkey. The three rented a house somewhere in the country, then my son went off the phone grid. I continued to call his number and either a voice replied, *'this number is not accessible'* or there was no reply at all!

In sheer desperation, I eventually rang the Australian Embassy in Turkey, and told them what I was experiencing.

Nothing happened. About three or four weeks later, I had a phone call from my son. From memory, his plane had just landed in Sydney, Australia. Answering the phone, I heard his wonderful voice, *'hi mum, how are you?'* I have never felt more relieved, than ever before to hear his wonderful voice.

The story went like this, and which I heard much later and well after his return to Australia, '...from Turkey, he had caught a plane to Israel and then made his way to Palestine. His reply to my question, *'Why did you go to Palestine?'* He said, *'to enhance my studies!'* He was doing advanced political studies. He had taken many photographs of situations he had seen, somehow, he had hidden the photographs in his luggage. On returning to the Israel Border, he was interrogated by Israeli Police for six or seven hours. The photographs were not found.

When he was a lot older, he told me the complete story, I then asked, *'Would you do it again?'* he answered, *'Not when I think about it, no, I would not.'*

YOUR EXTRA NOTES

UNDERSTANDING HOW THE HUMAN BODY GROWS AND MATURES & RELATIONSHIPS

This is a storybook for the young adult, also used as a reader for groups or in classroom settings.

HORMONES WITH HATS
CURRICULUM OBJECTIVES – UNITED KINGDOM (UK)

Natural body changes for boys between School Years 7 to 9, ages 11-14 years.

(Health and Wellbeing, Relationships, and Living in the Wider World)

Relationships Education, Relationships and Sex Education (RSE) and Health Education.

'Effective RSE does not encourage early sexual experimentation. It should teach young people to understand human sexuality and to respect themselves and others. It enables young people to mature, build their confidence and self-esteem and understand the reasons for delaying sexual activity. Effective RSE also supports people, throughout life, to develop safe, fulfilling, and healthy sexual relationships, at the appropriate time.'[2]

CURRICULUM OBJECTIVES – AUSTRALIA

Incorporating and supporting Year 7-9, ages 11-14 years. Personal, Social and Community Health (ACPPS070 – ACPS076 - ACPPS071 - ACPPS072 - ACPPS073 – and other related areas of the Curriculum including: TLF-IDM021182 Scootle.edu.au).

---

[2] Relationships and Sex Education (RSE) (Secondary) - GOV.UK (www.gov.uk) Extracted from 'statutory guidance Relationships Education, Relationships and Sex Education (RSE) and Health Education & Australia: https://www.scootle.edu.au

ONLINE SCHOOL PACKAGES

Full Potential Training offers a range of education packages. With our school packages for 'CHANGES', Children Growing Up, we cover the sensitive area of puberty and the changes that naturally occur in males and females. The story book at the beginning of each book allows the child to become familiar with the role that hormones play in making these body changes happen.

For young males with the ages of eleven to fourteen, we have developed, 'CHANGES' Facing Jai. The girls' book is 'Changes' Facing Caitlin. The books have been developed with discretion and to allow the child to quietly absorb the story board about the changes they are either going through or about to go through. We cover many sensitive areas of the subject of puberty, and how the female and male body works as the change occurs.

We offer a complete online package, which includes the story book. The online education packages do include the changes that both males and females go through during the time of puberty. They are not directed to one sex but both males and females. Once ordered, the package is downloaded from our server to the school, college, or holiday programme at your location.

The Package for Changes, Females and Males, Children between the ages of 11-14 has four by one-hour sessions, including a continuous 'voice over' with each slide. There are pause times for discussion and some question-and-answer sequences.

We ask that courses be ordered at least two (2) months in advance, this allows us to print and deliver the children's books to your location and in time for the lessons.

The package meet (please see page 107), both the Australian and United Kingdom objectives within Social Community Health and Relationship and Sex Education.

For more information, please email,

admin@fullpotentialtraining.com.au

Or, see our website, www.fullpotentialtraining.com.au

FAMILY PACKAGES

For many people, discussing puberty and the 'Changes' that take place within the human body are private discussions. They may not be easy discussions to have, but it is a necessary part of a parent's responsibility to their child or children.

For those people, we have developed Family Packages that include one book and a CD that is the same as the School Package.

If this allows you to discuss this topic with your family in private, please contact, admin@fullpotentialtraining.com.au

www.ingramcontent.com/pod-product-compliance
Lightning Source LLC
Chambersburg PA
CBHW062038290426
44109CB00026B/2665